Tantric Ethics

TANTRIC ETHICS

AN EXPLANATION OF THE PRECEPTS FOR BUDDHIST VAJRAYĀNA PRACTICE

TSONGKHAPA

TRANSLATED BY GARETH SPARHAM

FOREWORD BY JEFFREY HOPKINS

WISDOM PUBLICATIONS • BOSTON

Wisdom Publications, Inc.
199 Elm Street
Somerville MA 02144 USA
www.wisdompubs.org

Library of Congress Cataloging-in-Publication Data

Tsoṅ-kha-pa Blo-bzaṅ-grags-pa, 1357–1419.
Tantric ethics : an explanation of the precepts for Buddhist Vajrayana practice / Tsongkhapa ; translated by Gareth Sparham ; foreword by Jeffrey Hopkins. — 1st Wisdom ed.
p. cm.
Includes bibliographical references and index.
"The full title is: Fruit clusters of siddhis, an explanation of the way Bodhisattvas following the Bodhisattva's way of life by means of secret mantra should make their training in morality completlely pure"—Pref.
ISBN 0-86171-290-0 (pbk. : alk. paper)
1. Spiritual life—Tantric Buddhism—Early works to 1800. 2. Buddhist ethics—Early works to 1800. 3. Tantric Buddhism—Discipline—Early works to 1800. 4. Buddhism—China—Tibet—Doctrines—Early works to 1800. I. Sparham, Gareth. II. Title.
BQ7950.T754T37 2005
294.3'5—dc2 22005016789

First Wisdom Edition
ISBN 0-86171-290-0

09 08 07 06 05
5 4 3 2 1

Cover Art: Tsong Khapa, Chahar, Inner Mongolia, c.1700. Gilt brass, with pigments. Folkens Museum Etnografiska, Stockholm. Photograhy by John Bigelow Taylor, NYC.
Cover and interior design by Gopa &Ted2, Inc. Set in Sabon 9.8/14 pt.

Wisdom Publications' books are printed on acid-free paper and meet the guidelines for permanence and durability set by the Council of Library Resources.

Printed in the United States of America.

Table of Contents

Publisher's Acknowledgment

THE PUBLISHER gratefully acknowledges the generous help of the Hershey Family Foundation in sponsoring the printing of this book.

Foreword

TSONGKHAPA LOBSANG DRAGPA (1357–1419) is one of the most gifted philosophers and religious leaders produced by Tibet's Buddhist culture. In his *Great Exposition of Secret Mantra,* his seminal discourse on the practice of tantra, Tsongkhapa refers readers wishing to understand the crucial topic of tantric morality to another of his works, *Explanation of Tantric Morality Called "Fruit Clusters of Siddhis."* That text is the subject of the present book.

The tantric vows merit separate treatment both for their importance and for their complexity. Without keeping the vows, the sought-after results of tantric practice are impossible to achieve, and so understanding what these commitments entail is crucial. The complexity lies in the many cryptic terms used to enumerate and explain the vows as well as in the divergent traditions of commentaries on their meaning. Tsongkhapa addresses these points in detail, yielding a rich picture of the Indian sources and a nuanced explanation of this cornerstone of tantric practice.

In *Tantric Ethics,* Gareth Sparham's lucid translation and introduction make this essential material available to practitioner and scholar alike. Only a scholar with his long familiarity with Tibetan religious life and Buddhist doctrine could be a reliable guide to this treasure. It is with pleasure that I highly recommend this work to interested readers.

Jeffrey Hopkins
University of Virginia

Preface

I BEGAN WORK on this book more than twenty-five years ago in McLeod Ganj, India, with Denma Locho Rinpoche, a tantric guru distinguished as such both in terms of social status (he is recognized by Tibetans to be the reincarnation of an earlier tantric adept) and in terms of the personal effort he devotes to his practice. He read through the text with me and answered many questions that I put to him about it. I wish to thank him and acknowledge him as the senior collaborator in this project. I was also helped at that time by Lobsang Gyatso, a dear friend and mentor, and by many other learned Tibetan lamas. I am grateful for their generosity of spirit and thank them for their help.

I set the rough draft that I had produced aside for many years with the hope that Professor Jeffrey Hopkins or one of his students at the University of Virginia might make use of my notes to bring out an authentic translation. When it became clear that others were too busy, I returned to the work in the mountains in Dharmkot, above McLeod Ganj, in the early 1990s, a very lucky period of my life. I thank the Tibetan meditators and scholars who helped me in those years, and the Gaddi villagers there for making me welcome. I am also grateful to Nga-hua Yeo of West Vancouver, Canada, for her kindness as a benefactor to me as a monk during those years. I returned again to complete the project a few years ago in Ann Arbor, Michigan, carefully revising the translation and writing a new introduction. I would like to thank the scholars and staff of the Department of Asian Languages and Cultures at the University of Michigan, where I work teaching Tibetan language. In particular, I thank Professor Donald Lopez for his consistent support.

I also thank the editors at Wisdom Publications: first Dr. Nicholas Ribush for insisting that I publish this work with Wisdom, second Dr. Gene Smith, who pushed for necessary improvements in the text, and finally the present editors who have guided the book to publication.

Finally, I would like to thank Professor Jeffrey Hopkins. The catalyst for my work on this text was his translation of Tsongkhapa's *Ngagrim Chenmo,* published as *Tantra in Tibet* and *Yoga in Tibet.* I have never had the good fortune to study formally with Professor Hopkins, and he has not been involved in the preparation of this translation, but he was a benefactor and friend to me as a monk and student when I returned from India to do graduate work at the University of British Columbia in the 1980s, and he always welcomed me to his home. I am inspired by his enlightened attitude toward scholarship.

Introduction

> Comparing the proscriptions and prohibitions between the higher and lower vehicles and between the sūtra and tantra, one finds many dissimilarities. For those who are confused and lack the power of intelligence to seek the intended meaning of the innumerable scriptures, that these are all the practices of a single person is contradictory. Yet, through wisdom, the learned know that these are not mutually exclusive. There are limitless things the unwise see as contradictory and the wise know to lack contradiction.
>
> —Tsongkhapa, *Lamrim Chenmo*

> Morality does not become pure unless darkness is dispelled by the light of wisdom.
>
> —Āryaśūra, *Pāramitāsamāsa* 6.5

The Origin of the Text

This book presents for the first time in English translation a text on Buddhist tantric morality by Tsongkhapa (1357–1419). The full title is *Fruit Clusters of Siddhis: An Explanation of the Way Bodhisattvas Following the Bodhisattva's Way of Life by Means of Secret Mantra Should Make Their Training in Morality Completely Pure,* which I refer to simply as *Fruit Clusters.* When was it written? Khedrub Pelzangpo (1385–1438), a student of Tsongkhapa, writes in his biography of his teacher called *Stream of Faith* that Tsongkhapa dictated three books on Prātimokṣa, Mahāyāna, and tantric morality all about the same time, in the early years of the fifteenth century. According to Khedrub, in the early spring of 1402 at the request of the Drigung Kagyu hierarch, Tsongkhapa, Rendawa, and Kyabchog Pelzangpo spent the 1402 rains retreat at the old temple and monastery of Ar Jangchub Yeshe at Namtsedeng, near Drigung. Tsongkhapa's book on Prātimokṣa morality (mainly the morality for Buddhist monks and nuns) is called *Namtsedengma,* "the texts for, or written at, or reflecting the practice at Namtsedeng temple," and seems to originate from that event.[1]

After the rains retreat, Tsongkhapa went to Reting, where he finished his well-known *Lamrim Chenmo* in 1403. The colophons to his texts on Mahāyāna and tantric morality *(Basic Path to Awakening* and *Fruit Clusters)* and the colophon to the *Lamrim Chenmo* are all similar: They say that they were composed at Reting at the request of the Drigung hierarch and Kyabchog Pelzangpo.[2] It therefore appears likely that the *Fruit Clusters* was written at this time.

That Tsongkhapa's books on Prātimokṣa, Mahāyāna, and tantric morality are a set and were written at about the same time is important. It suggests that the three books together form a *domsum* ("three vows" or "codes"), or, at the least, a comment on this distinctly Tibetan literary genre. Mark Tatz, in the introduction to his excellent translation of *Basic Path to Awakening* (Tsongkhapa's explanation of the morality chapter of the *Bodhisattva Levels*), remarks that "it is equivalent to works of the Three Vows genre."[3] And the recent publication in China of a Tibetan edition of Tsongkhapa's three works on morality in two companion volumes accompanied by a polemical Three Vows work by Khedrub *(Brief Presentation and Determination of the Three Vows)* also seems to have been prompted, in part at least, by the same insight.[4]

The definitive three vows text is the brilliant, polemical *Explanation of the Three Codes* (Rhoton 2002) by Sakya Pandita (1182–1251). It is an expansion on shorter explanations of Mahāyāna and tantric morality by Sakya Pandita's uncle, Dragpa Gyelsten (1147–1216), and also, perhaps, a defense of his uncle's work against the criticisms of Vibhūticandra, a minor Indian pandit fluent in Tibetan (fl. ca. 1200). Vibhūticandra, while staying at Drigung Monastery, a seat of opposition to Sakya, wrote a short, but influential work, *Light Garland of the Three Codes,* critical of some of Dragpa Gyelsten's views.[5]

The first systematic commentaries on *Explanation of the Three Codes* appear toward the end of the fourteenth century, that is, in the period immediately before Tsongkhapa wrote his three texts on morality. During the later years of Tsongkhapa's life, and after his death, many commentaries on *Explanation of the Three Codes* appeared. It may be that during this time writing a three vows commentary was a sign of loyalty to the Sakya hierarchs. Tsongkhapa himself may have been consciously recognizing the importance of Sakya Pandita when he wrote his separate works on morality, which he understood as a work in the three vows tradition. Considered from the perspective of who his teachers were and the monasteries with which he had connection, and even the authors he cites as authoritative, it is not unhelpful to classify the historical Tsongkhapa as part of a Sakya tradition, at the very least to balance a putative history privileging the monolithic Gelug narrative found in the later hagiographies of Tsongkhapa.

It is also possible, however, that Tsongkhapa consciously wrote his explanations of Prātimokṣa, Mahāyāna, and tantric morality separately, and by doing so may have been making a critical comment about the structure of the three vows genre as it is found in *Explanation of the Three Codes* and its commentaries. His projection of the peripatetic Atiśa (982–1054) as the perfect guru at the start of his *Lamrim Chenmo,* written at the same time, may have been a conscious effort to move away from the projection of Sakya Pandita as the perfect guru.

This would solve many historical problems, but it is not an interpretation without difficulties. If true, you would expect early companions of Tsongkhapa to be aware of his intention, and that his intention would be reflected in their writings. In particular you would expect that Khedrub, the author of a number of polemical works directed against Rongton (1367–1449), an important Sakya writer critical of Tsongkhapa's views, would explicitly mention this fact.

It is significant, I think, that even Khedrub's own three vows text contains no clear indication that the three works by Tsongkhapa taken together are a comment on the shortcomings of the three vows genre, or an oblique criticism of Sakya Pandita. Khedrub says explicitly[6] that the main purpose of his text is to "get rid of some wrong opinions" about the three vows, but he criticizes the views expressed in Vibhūticandra's *Light Garland of the Three Codes* not Sakya Pandita's *Explanation of the Three Codes.* He says that to understand in more detail readers should consult "the works of my *Jetsun Lama Tsongkhapa,*" and that to understand bodhisattva morality the reader should consult "My guru lord, the omniscient one's explanation of the *[Bodhisattva Levels]* morality chapter," but he also respectfully cites Sakya Pandita himself as the "Dharma lord."[7]

The Topic and Tsongkhapa's Sources

The topic, or subject matter, of the *Fruit Clusters* is tantric morality. To discuss Buddhist tantric morality with at least some degree of clarity requires at the outset a definition of what Buddhist tantric morality is.

Following Tsongkhapa, I take it to be a system, in the sense of Christian morality, Confucian morality, or Islamic morality. As such, it is found, if it is to be found at all, in the Buddhist tantras (the literature). It is not discovered by examining the mores or practices of contemporary communities of Indians, Japanese, Bhutanese, Nepalese, or Tibetans who profess tantric Buddhist beliefs, any more than an investigation of the day-to-day behavior of American Southern Baptists would reveal Christian morality in this systematic sense. By the same token, within the residue of living communities of the past—their gravestones, architecture, and so forth—none will discover a system of Buddhist tantric morality. Of course such investigations produce valuable knowledge. But, as Max Nihom has pointed out somewhat acerbically, when it comes to the study of tantra in particular, a theoretically privileged (read, more scientific) knowledge from carefully sifted "realia," in contrast to a somehow less rigorous knowledge gleaned from high-status texts, is illusory. "The current interest in realia, Buddhist or Hindu, is but a high-status reflex of the academic study of pop-culture...Things of universal import are by any definition parcel of high, or elitist culture, while the import of realia is only recognizable after cognizance of the universalia to which they refer."[8] So the systematization of a people's observable actions and institutions may indeed convey knowledge, and that knowledge may be scientific, or at least have a scientific feel, but not only does it add nothing to our understanding of the normative beliefs of the elite conveyed in texts, it is, as a species of knowledge, equally confined to an elite, just a different one with a different interest.

Buddhist tantric morality, then, is narrowly defined as a systematic morality presented in a privileged series of texts. In *Fruit Clusters,* this morality is explained by way of an exhaustive commentary on four Indian Buddhist texts. The first of these Indian texts is the *Vajra Tip Tantra,* a supplement (explanation tantra) to the *Compendium of Principles Tantra.*[9] Historically, the *Compendium of Principles Tantra* is the pivotal text in the development of yoga and highest yoga tantras.[10] Still, this may not explain why Tsongkhapa used the *Vajra Tip Tantra* as his central text for the systematization of different tantric moral codes. It is still unclear whether the importance of the *Vajra Tip Tantra* derives specifically from Butön's (1290–1364) systematization of the yoga and highest yoga tantras during the formation of the Kangyur and Tengyur (the Buddhist canon in Tibetan translation), and hence from particular intellectual concerns dominant during the mid-fourteenth century, or if it derives from more basic considerations and the earlier importance of the yoga tantras in Tibet's religious and intellectual history.

The second half of *Fruit Clusters* is based on two small codifications of tantric rules *(Vajrayāna Root Downfalls* and *Vajrayāna Gross Downfalls).* A small section at the very end is based on a short passage from the consecration *(abhiṣekha)* chapter of the *Kālacakra Tantra*. The separate explanation of Kālacakra morality is probably the result of Tsongkhapa's well-known opposition to the views of the Jonangpa Dolpopa. In the Jonang tradition, the fusion of the Kālacakra tantra with general Mahāyāna Buddhism is a distinguishing feature.[11]

Many readers may know little about Buddhist tantric literature. The following brief overview, or map, of the literature Tsongkhapa cites is intended to give the reader a key to what may otherwise appear to be an arbitrary and bewildering array of sources.

As will become evident below, Tsongkhapa's explanation of tantric morality is structured on three interrelated views: (1) that tantric, five-family morality is the same in yoga and highest yoga tantras; (2) that there are different ordination rituals specific to the shared Bodhisattva Vehicle and the unshared Vajra Vehicle; and (3) that there is no exclusively tantric morality for the two lower action and performance sets of tantras, only bodhisattva morality.

Tsongkhapa's view that tantric ordination is the same in yoga and highest yoga tantras explains his choice of the *Vajra Tip Tantra* as his basic text, and it also explains the selection of Indian tantras and commentaries that he cites. As I said above, the *Compendium of Principles* (with the *Vajra Tip Tantra*) is, for Tsongkhapa, the basic yoga tantra, and he cites a number of important commentaries on it, among them Ānandagarbha's (fl. ca. 750) very long *Illumination of the "Compendium of Principles" Tantra* and Śākyamitra's (fl. ca. 750) major commentary, *Ornament of Kosala*. Tsongkhapa also frequently cites Ānandagarbha's *Maṇḍala Ritual Called Sarvavajrodaya* and the commentary on it by Munendrabhadra. The *Maṇḍala Ritual Called Sarvavajrodaya,* which is based on the

Compendium of Principles Tantra, is not a commentary but rather a ritual text based on its first chapter, the *Vajradhātu Maṇḍala*. To buttress his contention that tantric morality is the same across the entire range of yoga tantras, Tsongkhapa also cites the other two basic yoga tantras, the *Śrīparamādya Tantra* (with Ānandagarbha's extensive commentary on it) and the *Cleansing All States of Woe Tantra*.

Around these basic yoga tantra texts, Tsongkhapa arrays numerous extracts from highest yoga tantras—the *Guhyasamāja Tantra* group and the group of yoginī tantras, along with their commentaries and ritual texts. Even an informed reader can miss Tsongkhapa's intention at the outset. He cites the *Guhyasamāja Tantra* not directly, but obliquely through Śāntipa's explanation of a maṇḍala ritual by Dīpaṃkarabhadra. The reason Tsongkhapa's repeatedly cites Śāntipa's commentary is to include the *Guhyasamāja Tantra* in the early stages of his attempt to argue that the highest yoga tantras agree with the yoga tantras about the five family buddhas ordination.

The yoginī tantras that Tsongkhapa cites (and he often cites the tantras directly rather than a maṇḍala ritual or commentary) are the *Little Saṃvara Tantra* that he refers to as the root tantra, the *Vajraḍākinī Saṃvara Continuation Tantra, Saṃpuṭa Tantra, Ḍākārṇava Yoginī Tantra, Vajra Tent Tantra*, and *Buddhakapāla Tantra*. Although there are no doubt differences among these yoginī tantras, they are in *Fruit Clusters* to corroborate the assertion that the tantric morality set forth in the yoga tantras and in the *Guhyasamāja Tantra* is the same in the yoginī tantras as well. The extracts in later sections of *Fruit Clusters* from Abhayākaragupta's *Clusters of Quintessential Instructions* commentary on the *Saṃpuṭa Tantra*, and Bhavabhadra's commentary on the *Vajraḍāka Tantra* serve the same purpose, as do Tsongkhapa's frequent citations from the commentaries of Śāntipa and Nagpopa on the Vajrabhairava (Yamāntaka) tantra cycle (a smaller cycle incorporating elements of the Guhyasamāja and the yoginī tantras). He cites these latter two commentaries extensively when explaining the two small codifications of tantric rules, the *Vajrayāna Root Downfalls* and the *Vajrayāna Gross Downfalls*.

Overview of the Text

The *Fruit Clusters* begins with a citation from *Fifty Stanzas on the Guru:*

> Then they make you a receptacle for the good Dharma by giving you mantra and so forth. Then you should study the fourteen [tantric] root downfalls.

As for why the guru is such a central feature in tantric Buddhism, I think we should rather turn the question on its head and ask why a guru is not a central feature of Judaism, Christianity, and Islam. Clearly the religious teachers—the rabbis, the preachers, and the mullahs—are just as important institutionally in the day-to-day lives of followers of Semitic religions as are the gurus of tantric Buddhism. But it appears that the strong belief in God in those religions channels the stream of devotion awakened in the believer to the creator deity as the cultic center, rather than to the religious teacher him or herself. Practically speaking, there is little difference—without the stream of devotion, a person's religious life is a mere shell. If directing that stream of devotion to a creator god has the benefit of more easily awakening full admiration for the divine with all its infinite qualities, directing it toward an actual religious teacher, a guru, has the benefit of avoiding superstition.

Devotion to the guru, then, is a given for Tsongkhapa, as much as devotion to God is a given for Maimonides, Aquinas, or Muhammad. In the *Fruit Clusters*, as in his other works, Tsongkhapa stresses that the cultivation of devotion to a guru (or gurus) is particularly important not because deliverance is found through a power inhering in a deity or teacher, but because the path to deliverance and perfection is realized, in the first instance, by listening to and learning from experienced teachers, and then by practicing under their guidance. Tantric practice is esoteric and difficult, and thus the teacher plays a particularly vital role.

Because Tsongkhapa has given a detailed explanation of devotion to a tantric guru elsewhere,[12] he assumes that knowledge on the part of the reader and begins this text with a detailed explanation of the tantric ordination ritual proper. This ritual, says Tsongkhapa, is embedded in the consecration ritual section of the *Vajra Tip Tantra*. The participants here are the gurus, or tantric masters, who give the ordination, and the supplicants, or tantric yogis, who receive it.

The ritual begins with a section that proclaims the tantric morality to which the supplicants will commit themselves in the later part of the ordination ceremony. As Tsongkhapa says:

> Having proclaimed these pledges to be taken in order to make them known, with the intention to keep them, you take them by way of the ritual that I will explain below. In a word, when you take the vows, you take them within their being clearly delineated—not half-knowing, and half-not knowing them.

The morality proclaimed in the *Vajra Tip Tantra* (Vś) is systematized, in the first instance, as the specific points of morality of five family buddhas: Vairocana, Akṣobhya, Ratnasaṃbhava, Amitābha, and Amogha-siddhi. Vairocana represents the transformation of the form aggregate, Ratnasaṃbhava the transformation of the aggregate of feelings, Amitābha of naming, Amoghasiddhi of volitions, and Akṣobhya of consciousnesses.

The sūtras describe a person as five aggregates. The tantras describe a buddha as five buddhas. Both intend some form of the central Buddhist doctrine of selflessness. Sometimes this intention is clearly spelled out with an explicit discussion of selflessness, sometimes it is a text's unstated agenda. The unusual feature of tantric Buddhist descriptions of a buddha as five buddhas is that the selflessness is taken to be nondual with the "knowledge" *(jñāna)* that knows it.[13] By the middle of the nineteenth century, European writers already recognized the role of this nondual "knowledge" in tantric Buddhism:

> ...by five spontaneous acts of divine wisdom *(jnyān),* and by five exertions of mental reflection *(dhyān),* [are] created the Pancha-Dhyāni Buddha, or "Five Celestial Buddhas."[14]

In Tsongkhapa's explanation of tantric morality there is an unstated assumption that just as encountering any of the five *skandhas* is to encounter the person, to encounter the morality of any one family buddha is to encounter the morality of the central deity. Thus the morality of any one family buddha is the morality of any other, and all the moralities taken together are the morality of the primary buddha at the center of, or pervading, the maṇḍala.

Starting with the morality of the first of the five buddha families, the six points of Vairocana's morality are "refuge in the Three Jewels" (Vś 767.2) and what are called *the three moralities.* Refuge in the Three Jewels—the Buddha, Dharma, and Community—is morality in the sense that it incorporates behavior that accords with belief in the Three Jewels. The three moralities are "the training in morality, the morality that brings together wholesome dharmas, and the morality of working for the welfare of beings" (Vś 769.1–3). The three moralities derive from the Mahāyāna moralities set out by Asaṅga in the morality chapter of his *Bodhisattva Levels*. All three are an expansion on the morality *(śikṣā)* enjoined by *bodhicitta*, the thought/desire for enlightenment, which is an altruistic aspiration united with, or even identical to, the knowledge or wisdom of *jñāna*.

The "ethics of vows" (to use Mark Tatz's translation of the first Mahāyāna morality) is adherence to one of the seven Vinaya codes, beginning with the morality of the male and female householder, and ending with the morality of the fully ordained monk and nun. To interpret the "ethics of the vow" as a vowed morality, and the remaining two paths of Mahāyāna morality—the morality that brings together wholesome dharmas and the morality of working for the welfare of beings—as relating only to general attitude or prayer is wrong.[15] All three are vowed morality.

The third Mahāyāna morality is the vow *(saṃvara)* or pledge *(samaya)* to do all actions dictated by basic altruism: to give to the poor, the hungry, and so forth. The second is the morality that brings together wholesome dharmas, that is, the infinite dharmas ("qualities") that go into the composition of a perfect buddha. The enlightenment aspired to is premised on illusory realities (in the active sense of something dreamlike that beings find themselves caught up in) that, like didactic epiphanies, serve as ladders, as it is were, up which they climb onto the roof of freedom and the real. Hence the second of the three Mahāyāna moralities is unique to the Mahāyāna.

The morality of Vairocana incorporates all morality, as too do the moralities of the remaining four family buddhas. Still, the morality of each buddha encompasses a particular emphasis. Ratnasaṃbhava's morality is charity, codified as giving "the four gifts—of materials, fearlessness, doctrine, and love." Amitābha's morality is teaching, codified as demonstrating "the good Dharma—the external, secret, [and the] three vehicles." Amoghasiddhi's morality is to "keep perfectly possession of all the vows," and to cultivate worship. The *Vajra Tip Tantra* says of Akṣobhya's morality:

> The mahātmas shall also keep vajra, bell, and mudrā. They say the vajra is bodhicitta, the bell is wisdom. They shall also keep

> the masters' [vow]. Gurus are equal to all the buddhas. They say this is the pledge vow of the pure vajra family. [Vś 767.2–4]

I have already addressed the masters', or guru, vow. In reference to the other three, Tsongkhapa says:

> Authentically keeping a vajra and bell is keeping a symbolic vajra and bell, and, knowing the meaning they symbolize, holding the vajra and ringing the bell. This is keeping [them] by [keeping in mind] what they really are. Now, the nondual mind—the bodhicitta of all tathāgatas—is the secret or inner vajra. Keeping the external vajra, within recollecting that [inner vajra], is keeping the vajra by [keeping in mind] what it really is.

About the bell he says:

> Just as space, the mere negation of all obstructing matter, is not an entity with an own-being, similarly everything is without own-being because it is, ultimately, from its very start, unproduced. Suchness is comparable to, or like, space. Those uniting with that are yogis. Their minds and mental factors and true reality are one taste. The transcendental wisdom of those yogis therefore lights up or encompasses suchness, which is the supreme thing that is comparable in all. As [in Vś 767.3], "They say...wisdom is the bell," such wisdom is what the bell symbolizes, and even though one rings a symbolic bell, ringing it with the idea that one is sounding out statements like those is keeping [the bell pledge] by [keeping in mind] what it really is.

Finally, you keep the mudrā vow by modeling yourself after the state of perfect enlightenment in the form of a particular family buddha. As Tsongkhapa says, "As yogis in one or the other family, they arise in the form of Vairocana and so forth, purify [i.e., symbolically transform] their state as an [ordinary] being,[16] and recite mantra in meditation."

Together these constitute the family buddha pledges that are the codification of basic tantric morality.

The *Vajra Tip Tantra* does not proclaim in detail the general tantric code with fourteen major and eight secondary vows—that is, the code not systematized as specific points of morality of five family buddhas—but it does say that supplicants should avoid the "fourteen...root downfalls." This is enough for Tsongkhapa to argue that this text does in fact proclaim the general code as well, and that supplicants take those vows as part of the consecration in both yoga and highest yoga tantra.

Because the *Vajra Tip Tantra* does not explicitly detail the points of the general code, Tsongkhapa necessarily bases his explanation of these on a different text, the *Vajrayāna Root Downfalls.* Readers of *Fruit Clusters* should know that Tsongkhapa's decision to explain the fourteen general tantric vows only after he has finished explaining the entire tantric ordination ritual is necessitated by textual, not theoretical considerations. It is because the *Vajra Tip Tantra* does not detail each of the fourteen general tantric vows separately, not because Tsongkhapa understands the general code to be separate from the ordination ritual. Readers should also know that the morality of the general code is proclaimed during the earlier part of the ordination ritual, and that the vows are then taken in the later part, along with the family buddha pledges.

The *Vajrayāna Root Downfalls* says the first downfall is disparaging your gurus. The reason we have to consider our teachers the highest field of worship and revere them is not because they are gods, but because they are the door to tantric practice. After receiving consecration and learning tantra from them, thinking "There is nothing in this" leads to the first root downfall. The second is knowingly and willfully breaking a promise to keep any of the Prātimokṣa, Mahāyāna, or tantric moralities demonstrated by the buddhas, motivated by the wish to willfully ignore them. The third is hating somebody consecrated and ordained by the same tantric guru, and, cognizant of that "relationship," saying something cruel to them. These first three downfalls are connected with refuge in the Buddha, Dharma, and Community, respectively.

The fourth and fifth downfalls are giving up love for beings and giving up bodhicitta. Both encapsulate the essence of Mahāyāna morality. "Sixth is criticizing the doctrine of your own or other tenet systems."[17] Tsongkhapa restricts the scope of the vow to all Buddhist systems, and he understands criticizing to mean deprecating from the bottom of your heart with the thought "The Buddha never said that." The implication is that Buddhist fundamentalism—the restriction of the canon to a very limited number of books saying the same thing—is an appropriate morality for those of a "Hīnayāna" persuasion but a great immorality for those following tantra.

Thus the seventh rule is "speaking publicly about secrets to immature beings,"[18] since they do not have faith in esoteric Buddhism, and speaking about it openly will only drive them further away.

The eighth downfall "is treating the aggregates that are in essence the five buddhas with contempt."[19] This does not mean rejecting meditations on uncleanliness, because the *Vajra Tip Tantra* says explicitly that, "Those with a longing for sex should remove it by meditation on ugliness." Rather this downfall refers to torturing yourself with flagellation or any other extreme austerity intended to injure your body or mind.

The ninth downfall is not making the emptiness taught in nontantric Mahāyāna texts a central tenet of belief and understanding, and the eleventh is giving up such belief and understanding after finding it.

The tenth downfall is not resorting to violence when the situation requires it. This, and the twelfth downfall, "repulsing the minds of living beings who have faith,"[20] make it abundantly clear that tantric morality is a code for a spiritual elite. It is wrong not to praise and teach tantra when students are from good families, have been properly educated, and are genuinely altruistic. To praise and teach Prātimokṣa morality exclusively, uninformed by Mahāyāna and tantric morality, to such students is a downfall. Similarly, if the very highest saints make a dogma even of Mahāyāna peace and altruism it is a downfall.

The last two downfalls are "not resorting to pledges as they are found," and "despising women whose essence is wisdom."[21] For an explanation of both the reader should consult the relevant sections in *Fruit Clusters*.

Breaking Vows

In Prātimokṣa morality, supplicants are accepted into the Buddhist order of monks and nuns. If, at a later time, they break a basic rule entailing expulsion from the order—to refrain from murder, sex, and so forth—they are expelled, in essence, excommunicated. Such excommunication was meaningful both for those excommunicated and for those doing the excommunicating, the former because they could no longer avail themselves of the prestige of others in the order when they begged for food or performed rituals and so on, and the latter because their appeals to the laity based on their morality and ritual competence would no longer be compromised by the behavior of those excommunicated.

In contrast, however, the tantric Buddhist order rarely, if ever, followed such a standard, even if the ordination ceremony outlined in *Fruit Clusters* suggests otherwise. As with the Mahāyāna, the tantric order is largely populated not by ordinary humans with an ordinary ethical standard, even such a noble one as that encoded in the Prātimokṣa, but by beings whose morality entitles them to such names as "celestial" *(deva)* and "elite" *(ārya)*. Such beings may live in any part of the universe, and they may or may not be living in communities. Hence a fall from Mahāyāna or tantric morality does not result in excommunication in the Prātimokṣa sense. Nevertheless it results in an "expulsion" from the order in the sense that their morality is no longer the morality of a member of a spiritual elite. In this narrow sense those guilty of immorality commit a downfall and are expelled and excommunicated.

In the Prātimokṣa there is a codification of behavior that does not actually entail expulsion from the order but is nevertheless reprehensible to a greater or lesser degree. So too in the tantric code. Tsongkhapa brings in this sort of behavior in tantra under the rubric "branch pledges" and "gross infractions." Included within the branch pledges are the rules for what you must not do, and the rules for what you must do. The *Vajra Tip Tantra* says:

> You should not kill the living, nor take what is not given, nor engage in perverted pleasures. And you should not tell a lie. Give up that root of all ruination, alcoholic beverages. Except to tame living beings, give up everything that should not be done. [Vś 768.1–3]

In reference to the positively framed branch pledges, the *Vajra Tip Tantra* says, "To the extent of your abilities you should cultivate the three physical actions, the four actions of speech, and the three actions of mind" (Vś 768.3–4). Thus supplicants in the tantric ordination ritual commit to keep not only the pledges of the five family buddhas and the fourteen general tantric vows, but also basic Prātimokṣa householder morality, and the even more basic ten wholesome action paths *(daśakuśalakarmapatha)*.

The apparent contradiction between these branch vows and the general root tantric vows is only a superficial one. Consider, for example, the vow to refrain from abstaining from violent behavior. The logic of tantric morality understands murder and breaking a Prātimokṣa rule to be close to the tantric root downfall of abstaining from violent behavior when called for. If, after taking the tantric morality ordination ritual, the person breaks the Prātimokṣa rule against murder with the notion that it is not a Buddhist rule that must be strictly followed (tantric downfall number two and thirteen), without caring that it is a vow of Vairocana (pledge number four), or without caring that it is also a pledge of Amitābha and Amoghasiddhi, it would constitute a full tantric downfall.

Again, readers should recall that Tsongkhapa explains the eight gross tantric infractions after he has finished explaining the entire tantric ordination ritual because of textual, not theoretical considerations. In the *Vajra Tip Tantra,* beyond the passages cited above, there is only an exhortation to supplicants to desist from behavior degrading to the maṇḍala, guru, and the symbols of practice. Still, Tsongkhapa takes this brief section as a proclamation of the gross infractions and then explains them in detail later.

The Ordination

In the *Vajra Tip Tantra* the ordination proper begins with a request from the supplicants, "Sage, Sun, Fully Enlightened Being, please turn your thoughts to me, please grant me ordination" (Vś 766.1–7).

The presiding teacher asks if the supplicants want to take the ordination or not, "Do you wish, noble one, to keep the secret of those in the great secret family?" (Vś 766.7–767.1) and then gives the ordination, modeling the words, which the supplicants repeat three times, beginning with, "Just as the lords during the three periods of time were set on enlightenment, so too shall I produce the unequalled and supreme bodhicitta" (Vś 768.7–769.1).

The presiding teacher then gives each of the five family buddha pledges individually and concludes with the statement, "Having produced the highest, supreme bodhicitta, I will keep all vows for the sake of all living beings. I will free those not free, liberate those not liberated, give relief where there is no relief, and place living beings in nirvāṇa."

Having completed the explanation of the ordination ritual, Tsongkhapa, in chapter 3 of the English translation, addresses two questions: first, are all supplicants who are allowed into any part of a consecration ritual consecrated, and second, do all those who receive tantric consecration receive a tantric ordination? The answer to both questions is no. This is the essence of the three subsections of chapter 3 in Tsongkhapa's text, "[1] not consecrating those not taking vows, [2] having dealt with those objections, taking the vows through consecration, and [3] identifying which vows are taken in action and performance tantra consecrations."

The Buddhist tantras are many, and they are systematized into four sets: action, performance, yoga, and highest yoga tantra. For each tantra there is a corresponding consecration ritual. There are many of these rituals as well, and each includes two basic sections: a preliminary section and the consecration itself. In the former, those to be consecrated are led into the *maṇḍala*—the transformed environment and inhabitants—and in the latter they are consecrated inside the maṇḍala. Hence consecration rituals are often called maṇḍala rituals *(maṇdalavidhi, maṇḍalopāyika)*. The core of the preliminary section includes a first section called "entering in," in which supplicants enter from the east, circumambulate, and bow to the deity. That is followed by the "giving solemn promise" section, in which supplicants request ordination. That is followed by the "pledge and wisdom being indivisible" and "fixing [the resolve]" sections, in which they give their word as a pledge and garlands are offered to them.

There are some people who only participate in the "entering in" part of the ritual. This entering in is allowed because of the general conception that tantra is greatly beneficial to the minds of beings, as it produces an irreversible intention to become enlightened for the sake of others more quickly. Hence it is good to stimulate the interest of persons who have only a casual interest by allowing them to participate in the first part of the consecration, without enjoining on them any moral code at all. In these cases, teachers do not discriminate, and do not conduct a careful investigation of the interests and capacities of these participants, but simply let them partake in the ritual up until the end of the first part of the preliminary section. This is true of all consecrations, even highest yoga tantra consecration, and is called "letting them enter the maṇḍala." Hence there are some supplicants who seem to be involved in a consecration ritual but are not.

Just as the preliminary section of the consecration ritual is subdivided into sections, so too is the consecration proper. It includes an earlier section (up to but not including the five family buddha ordination) called the *disciple consecration section*, and a later section, beginning with the five family buddha ordination, called the *master consecration section*.

Do all true supplicants (not those who are given mere entry into the maṇḍala for auspicious purposes) participate in the entire consecration ritual, both the disciple consecration and the master consecration sections? No, they do not. Hence all supplicants do not take the five family buddha ordination. All true supplicants, even those not suited to the master consecration who take only the disciple consecration, do take an ordination, however, because a consecration in the absence of an ordination has no meaning. Hence those participating in only the disciple consecration sections take a Mahāyāna ordination, also called the bodhisattva vows. In essence these are comprised of the three Mahāyāna moralities discussed earlier. The "unshared" tantric ordination of the five family buddhas is reserved for those taking the master consecration.

In regard to the correspondence between the disciple and master consecrations, and the ordinations "shared" and "not shared" with non-tantric Mahāyāna, Tsongkhapa says:

> Those with just disciple consecration are those who, whether or not they strive for consecration as a master, take only the shared ordination and do not take the master ordination...those striving for master consecration and those striving for just disciple consecration both have to take refuge-based bodhicitta vows. These are therefore shared or general vows. The five family vows taken with the passage that begins, "Just as the lords of the three times..." [Vś 769.2–3] are not, however, given when it is just a disciple consecration, [424] but are given in master consecrations.

The final section of chapter 3 of this translation ("which vows are taken in action and performance tantra consecrations") further explains that the master consecration has two different meanings within the consecration ritual. It may be the name for the part of the consecration after the knowledge consecration but before the master consecration proper, or it may be the true master consecration, which is reserved for those taking the five family buddha ordination.

The knowledge consecration is subdivided into a water, headdress, vajra, and bell consecration, and so on. These consecrations are collectively called *knowledge consecration* because they "cause the antidote to ignorance to become effective." All are part of the disciple consecration. The irreversible consecration, secret consecration, permission, prophecy, reliefs, and praise that follow the knowledge consecration and complete the disciple consecration stage are the *six particulars*. These are sometimes called a *master consecration* because they permit supplicants to draw the maṇḍala and demonstrate the doctrine. In the action and performance tantras, the consecration proper consists only of the knowledge consecration and the "six-particular master consecration." Hence in these two lower tantra sets there is no true master consecration, and supplicants do not take the five family buddha ordination, only bodhisattva vows.

The true master consecration is subdivided into the vase, secret, knowledge, and word consecrations reserved for yoga and highest yoga tantras, which follow the disciple consecration. It requires the supplicant to take not only the bodhisattva vows, but the five family buddha ordination as well.

What, then, is the Mahāyāna morality, the bodhisattva vows, that supplicants in action and performance tantras take? Tsongkhapa says it is the same morality taught to bodhisattvas in the *Bodhisattva Levels,* the *Ākāśagarbha Sūtra,* and the *Skillful Means Sūtra,* which he explains at length in his *Basic Path to Awakening*. He says that the four root downfalls in that moral code are forsaking the Dharma, giving up bodhicitta, being miserly, and harming living beings. Readers should consult the relevant parts of *Fruit Clusters* and *Basic Path to Awakening* to learn more about these.

Root Downfalls

The *Vajra Vehicle Root Downfalls* is a short explanation of the fourteen points of the general code that is said to be composed by Aśvaghoṣa or, in the Tibetan colophon of Tsongkhapa's text, "the master Bha-bi-lha." In his detailed commentary on it, comprising most of the second half of *Fruit Clusters,* Tsongkhapa examines in more detail what the "object" is in each downfall and what act constitutes the downfall.

In explaining the first downfall, "disparaging" tantric masters, he investigates who the guru, the "object" of the downfall, is. Does the guru have to have taught the student; if so, for how long? Does the guru have to have given a consecration, and, if so, how high a consecration, and so on. He says the first downfall is incurred when disciples think nothing special of what they have heard from a tantric guru, be it a consecration or even the tiniest bit of advice about a tantric practice, and, getting irritated, ridicule the guru who gave it to them.

To be a downfall this has to be not just a single outburst, but a decided heartfelt opinion, and the opinion has to come to mind again and again and be deemed right and just, and has to be accompanied by a feeling of pleasure. Futher, to be a complete downfall there must never be any regret for it. These are what Asaṅga in his explanation of the bodhisattva vows calls "greater involvement."

Tsongkhapa directs the reader to his explanation of bodhisattva morality in *Basic Path to Awakening,* where he says that bodhisattvas totally break a bodhisattva vow only when they do it without any conscience and without any concern for the disadvantages, and when they look forward to doing it again in the future and being pleased with what they have done. Tsongkhapa adds that "these [two] absences, furthermore, must be absences from the second instant after the motivation of the downfall up to the moment right before the completion of the actual deed, and the [two] presences must be present during that period as well. If there is a lack of any one of the absences or presences, there is no defeat." This is the case for all fourteen downfalls with the exception of the fifth, "giving up bodhicitta." When the factors of greater involvement are not present there is a *gross* downfall, but not a *root* downfall. The same holds true for most of infractions of the vinaya and bodhisattva codes as well.

The second downfall is when yogis "overstep the words of the sugatas." Tsongkhapa restricts this downfall to treating a rule from any of the three codes of conduct as unimportant and breaking it. This leaves room for a meaningful delineation of the sixth downfall, "criticizing the doctrine of your own and other tenet systems," which he restricts to belittling any doctrine in the Listener, Pratyekabuddha, Perfection, or Vajra Vehicle as silly and saying it is not a teaching of the Buddha. Tsongkhapa makes the important point that to break this vow you have to actively criticize the statement and insist it is not a teaching of the Buddha. There is no fault in simply recognizing a particular doctrine or belief for what it is and not believing it.

The third downfall happens if, motivated by hatred, you say something cruel to a fellow practitioner consecrated by the same guru and in possession of tantric vows. For it to be the full downfall you have to be cognizant of who the person is and their status, and the "relative" has to hear what you say and understand what you mean. "Vajra relatives" in this context are people related by having been admitted into the same maṇḍala by the same guru.

The fourth downfall is "giving up love for beings," that is, entertaining malice that wishes ill on any group or individual. The fifth is "giving up bodhicitta," a composite made up of a compassionate response to the suffering of others, and the solemn oath to perfect oneself in order to do all that can be done to relieve their suffering. Having made such a prayer, as it were, to give it up is unconscionable, and just doing so even for a moment is a downfall.

Tsongkhapa gives a very narrow definition of the seventh downfall, "speaking publicly about secrets." He says "when there is [1] someone who has not been matured by consecration, [2] someone in whom no faith arises when the secrets are proclaimed, and [3] you are cognizant of the fact, if [4] you talk about an unshared secret and [5] it is understood while [6] there is no great purpose—[such as the purpose of] taming others—then the six factors are complete, and the seventh root downfall [is incurred]." This downfall is defined differently relative to higher consecrations. Thus those who have the highest consecration break the vow by revealing those secrets even to practitioners with a yoga tantra consecration. Those in turn break the vow if they reveal their secrets to those consecrated in a tantra in the next set below, and so on.

The eighth downfall is incurred in two ways, by engaging in extreme religious austerities that harm the body, or by habituating to the view that the five aggregates are impure, as opposed to the five buddhas that are pure. Again, Tsongkhapa says that this vow should not be interpreted to mean that tantric practitioners should avoid meditating on the the body as ugly to counteract obsessive sexual craving.

To "doubt the essential purity of dharmas," which Tsongkhapa defines as actively not believing in selflessness or emptiness, is the ninth downfall. The "false imagination of dharmas without names" is the eleventh. This differs from the ninth because it occurs when, after attaining the correct view and being in a position to foster it, you let yourself fall into settling down on what is empty and dreamlike as real. This has to persist, Tsongkhapa suggests based on a statement by Atiśa, for twenty-four hours. Tsongkhapa says that fostering either the Middle Way or the Mind Only view is sufficient, and he specifically says the vow is not broken by a Middle Way or Mind Only tāntrika who strongly disagrees with another learned Buddhist's formulation of the view.

The tenth downfall is "persistently showing affection to the wicked," which means, in essence, killing them. Tsongkhapa says that such disturbing vows are "simply mentioned in the mantra. Consider them wrong and do not do them." He says those capable of such a vow would be so compassionate they could cause the victim to take rebirth in a buddha's pure land, could revivify the corpse of the victim with somebody else's consciousness, and would have a direct knowledge of all the victim's previous and future lives. Such exceptional saints engage in violent behavior to prevent their victims from having to experience interminable suffering in a state of woe when there is no other way to prevent them committing a crime. Tsongkhapa makes a particular point of stressing that even important, skilled politicians should not think they are given a dispensation to engage in violence. He recounts the story of Cānakya, the Mauryan prime minister who, even though a highly accomplished tāntrika, suffered terrible rebirths because of violent political strategy.

Twelfth is "repulsing the minds of living beings who have faith." Again, Tsongkhapa narrowly defines the downfall as occurring when "there is [1] a living being who is a suitable receptacle for the Mahāyāna who has faith in a particular supreme [Vajra]yāna guiding instruction, and [2] with a willful intention to arrest their desire-to-do, you [3] employ some means to cause mental repulsion, and [4] their desire-to-do stops."

Tsongkhapa says the thirteenth downfall is different in yoga tantra and highest yoga tantra. In yoga tantra, he says, the downfall of "not resorting to pledges" is incurred by practitioners who say that meditation is the main thing, and that the vajra, bell, and hand mudrā are ridiculous. Readers should consult the relevant section of this translation, and consult Snellgrove's translation of the *Hevajra Tantra* and the work of Chris George to understand how the downfall might occur for a practitioner of highest yoga tantra.

Finally, Tsongkhapa says you incur the fourteenth downfall if you find any fault with an enlightened goddess you mistake for an ordinary woman, or if you say something disparaging about women in general. From the perspective of a modern reader, he uses a most curious example to make his point.

After listing each of the downfalls, the *Vajra Vehicle Root Downfalls* says, "Mantric practitioners will definitely obtain siddhis if they avoid these. Otherwise they break their pledges. Broken, they are possessed by Māra. Then they experience suffering and wander facing down in hell." In his extensive commentary on this, Tsongkhapa explains how contemplating the benefit of keeping the ordination and the danger of breaking it is a crucial practice to prevent downfalls. He then explains how the best way to prevent a downfall from a bodhisattva vow or a tantric vow is to block four doors. The first door is not knowing what a downfall consists in. You block it by knowing well what the root and branch downfalls are. The second door is arrogance that precludes respect for friends who share the same ordination. It is blocked by conquering pride and respecting those friends. The third door is lacking in conscientiousness, mindfulness, and vigilance. That door is closed by listening to your conscience. And the final door to block is your dominant obsessions, be they an inflated sense of who you are, obsessive need for sexual pleasure, obsessive drive for status, or whatever leads to a downfall. You close that final door by counteracting the afflictive emotions that are dominant with the appropriate antidotes.

Finally, after criticizing those who fail to read widely in the tantras, and who base their tantric morality, or rather immorality, on a literal interpretation of just a few statements, he explains in some detail the way to repair downfalls with the Vajrasattva mantra and meditation.

Gross Downfalls

As stated earlier, *gross downfalls* are in essence root downfalls lacking in certain branches. Tsongkhapa bases his explanation of them on the *Vajra Vehicle Gross Downfalls* of "the master Nāgārjuna." Tsongkhapa says the eight given in the *Vajra Vehicle Gross Downfalls* are just examples. "Relative to the Vajrayana vows, it includes all the misdeeds other than the class that constitutes [root] downfalls."

The first gross downfall is "violently appropriating a wisdom woman." Tsongkhapa cites another short codification of gross downfalls said to be by Aśvaghoṣa that explains this as enjoying a knowledge woman where the woman has faith in tantra but has not been properly given access to the necessary consecrations and teaching that would allow her to understand and keep pledges. The gross downfall occurs when, within such an unbalanced relationship, you make fun of the woman or put the woman down.

This is similar to the Prātimokṣa code. For example, in the Prātimokṣa, full sexual relations entail expulsion. Traveling unaccompanied with a person of the opposite sex, sitting alone in a room with the windows closed with a person of the opposite sex, conveying a love note between a couple, and so on, are infractions that are gross, but do not entail expulsion. Similarly, in the tantric code, if a tantric adept keeping tantric pledges despises a woman because she is a woman, it entails expulsion. If the adept countenances any abusiveness toward a timid, unlearned pledge woman with faith, it is a gross downfall but does not necessarily entail complete expulsion.

The second gross downfall in the list, "violently appropriating her nectar," is similar. Even if the two pledge persons were equally consecrated, and had equal knowledge, pushing the knowledge woman into the activity at an inappropriate time, in front of people without faith, and so on, would be gross, but would not entail, as it were, the expulsion that the true prejudice of intellectual misogyny in a person who should know better entails.

The remaining six examples of a gross downfall: revealing tantric implements and pictures to those who would scoff at them, quarreling with vajra friends during a tantric celebration, teaching a Buddhist doctrine other than emptiness to somebody who would understand if you taught them emptiness, staying for more than a week with Buddhists who scoff at tantra, pretending to have deep insight into tantra when all you have done is a daily ritual evocation of a diety (Tsongkhapa says, "This is the sort of gross downfall we are prone to nowadays"), and teaching mantra secrets to those who scoff at tantra can be understood in the same way.

As I suggested above, Tsongkhapa probably explains the Kālacakra Tantra morality separately because of his opposition to the views of the Jonangpa Dolpopa. According to Tsongkhapa, the Kālacakra presentation of tantric morality differs in a number of ways from the standard presentation but is similar in its essentials. He cites a passage from the Kālacakra consecration chapter that lists not five, but seven, buddha family pledges and says that some of the Kālacakra pledges have the same names but mean different things. Furthermore, the last pledge, the pledge of the "producer of victory," is not found in other tantras at all.

Tsongkhapa cites another passage from the consecration chapter and gives a detailed commentary on it. In this passage the fourteen downfalls are each numbered traditionally. The second, for example, is called "the other," the tenth is called "directions," and so on. Tsongkhapa notes a difference between the first two downfalls here and the first two downfalls in the standard presentation. He also points out the difference in the way the Kālacakra explains the fifth and sixth downfalls. He says the Kālacakra defines the sixth downfall as making a qualitative distinction between the Perfection Vehicle and the Mantra Vehicle. The reader can consult the relevant section in the translation to examine these in more detail.

In the final section of *Fruit Clusters,* Tsongkhapa anticipates the insight section of his *Lamrim Chenmo,* where he says the middle way is between two extremes—one that negates too much and one that negates too little. Here he plots a tantric path between two extremes. The first extreme is over-emphasizing the collection of meritorious deeds and playing down the role of meditation on emptiness for achieving the state of a buddha. The second extreme is over-emphasizing the meditation on emptiness and playing down the collection of merits. He says the tantric path is a middle way between these two extremes, comprised both of a generation stage (the practice of deeds to accumulate merit) and a completion stage (the practice of nondual knowledge to accumulate wisdom). Through those you reach the level of Vajradhara.

Note on Translation

DOUBLE QUOTATION MARKS indicate words and phrases from a root text that Tsongkhapa is glossing. Numbers in square brackets are to the pages of the Tibetan text edited by Ngawang Geleg Demo, volume *ka*. Numbers in brackets preceded by the abbreviation Vś are to the Tibetan translation of the *Vajra Tip Tantra Vajra*, number 113 in the Peking edition of the Tibetan Kanjur. Numbers in brackets preceded by the abbreviation Mā and Sā are to the Sanskrit editions of the *Vajra Vehicle Root Downfalls* and the *Vajra Vehicle Gross Downfalls*, respectively, published by S. Lévi in his article "Autour d'Aśvaghoṣa." Words and phrases inside parentheses indicate a direct translation of foreign words. All titles of books are given only in an English translation equivalent, with original titles listed in the bibliography.

An Explanation of Tantric Morality Called "Fruit Clusters of Siddhis"

༄༅། གསང་སྔགས་ཀྱི་ཚུལ་ཁྲིམས་ཀྱི་རྣམ་བཤད་
དངོས་གྲུབ་ཀྱི་སྙེ་མ་ཞེས་བྱ་བ། །

TSONGKHAPA

ཙོང་ཁ་པ་བློ་བཟང་གྲགས་པ་

Tsongkhapa's Preface

Homage to Guru Mañjughoṣa.

THIS TEXT IS CALLED *Fruit Clusters of Siddhis*. It is an explanation of the way that bodhisattvas following the bodhisattva's way of life by means of secret mantra should make their training in morality completely pure.

> I reverently prostrate to the feet of the noble, holy compassionate ones.
>
> Glorious, all-pervading Vajrasattva, please take me to heart with your compassionate mind. As you do so, [the goddesses] Locanā and so forth bestow the finest consecration, the bodhisattvas proclaim auspicious verses clearly and pleasantly, the wrathful protector deities overcome the army of hindrances, and you bestow every magical and spiritual accomplishment *(siddhi)* on hosts of wanderers. Please take me to heart as your child and gather an ocean [379] of success for me without hindrance.

I shall explain, in accordance with the teachings of the wise, the way adepts who have entered the Vajrayāna are continually blessed by buddhas and bodhisattvas, and lovingly befriended by the ḍākinīs of the three places, keep pure the pledges and vows that, like the waxing moon, are the foundation for increasing good qualities. You who wish to progress in the profound Vajrayāna should listen respectfully, with a mind bowed in reverence.

The *Fifty Stanzas on the Guru* says:

> After this, having been made a receptacle for the holy Dharma by having been given mantra and so forth, read about the fourteen root downfalls, and abstain from them.

All those adepts who have received a stainless consecration, have been made into receptacles for tantra, and who want to travel the Vajrayāna path should, first of all, endeavor to keep the pledges and vows that are the root of both siddhis purely.[22] For as it says in the first chapter of the *Little Saṃvara Tantra:*

> Dispassionate adepts should always guard the pledges. When they break pledges they do not attain the siddhis that come from receiving consecration in a maṇḍala.

Also it says [380] in the seventh part of the *Vajraḍākinī Saṃvara Continuation Tantra:*

> Those who have not entered a mandala, have given up their pledges, and do not fully understand the secrets accomplish nothing, even after they have done the practice.

Thus it says that those who ignore and do not guard what is to be guarded—the pledges and so forth—do not attain any siddhis at all, even after they have followed the path. This is why I am going to explain the root and branch pledges of Vajrayāna practitioners here.

The explanation is in two parts: first, how their commitment to the pledges and vows comes about, and second, determining the downfalls that break the vows to which they have committed themselves.

1. Proclamation

THE FIRST has three parts: explanation of the proclamation of vows, explanation of taking vows, and the issue of which consecrations are to be bestowed when vows are or are not kept. The first of these has two parts: the specific pledges of the five families and the general pledges. The first of these has five parts: the pledges of the Vairocana, Akṣobhya, Ratnasaṃbhava, Amitābha, and Amoghasiddhi families, respectively.

Specific Pledges of the Five Families

Pledges of Vairocana

[The *Vajra Tip Tantra*] says:[23]

> Take refuge in the Three Jewels—the Buddha, Dharma, and Community. This is the firm pledge of the beautiful Buddha family. [Vś 767.2]

"Take refuge in the Three Jewels—the Buddha, Dharma, and Community" is a command. The "pledge of the Buddha" Vairocana "family" is like that. Although [381] many Indian texts have *dag* instead of *dga,*[24] *sangs rgyas rigs dga' ba'i* ["of the beautiful Buddha family"] is correct because Nagpochopa's two[25] *[Saṃvara* and *Mahāmāyā] Maṇḍala Rituals,* and Saroruha's *Maṇḍala Ritual* and so forth say, *dkon mchog gsum la skyabs su song / 'di ni sangs rgyas rigs yid 'ong* ("Take refuge in the Three Jewels / It is...the beautiful Buddha family"). It is "firm" means it is hard for the opposition to break it apart.

Pledges of Akṣobhya

> The great-minded shall also keep vajra, bell, and mudrā.[26] They say the vajra is bodhicitta and the bell is wisdom. They shall

> also keep the master's [vow]. Gurus are equal to all the buddhas. They say this is the pledge vow of the pure Vajra family. [Vś 767.2–4]

It proclaims that "the great-minded shall keep vajra, bell, and mudrā." What are those things that have to be kept? It teaches with "they say the vajra..." and so forth. I will explain these three in the section on keeping vows [406.6–409.2]. Not only should they keep these three, but they should also "keep the" vajra "master's" vow out of respect. This is because the benefits and faults that come from respecting or not respecting a guru are "equal" or similar to respecting or not respecting all the buddhas. Thus the victors "say this," [say that] keeping those four "is the pledge" and "vow of the" completely "pure Vajra" Akṣobhya "family."

As for the difference between these two, [the pledge and vow,] in Śāntipa's *Commentary on [Dīpaṃkarabhadra's] Guhyasamāja Maṇḍala Ritual* in four hundred and fifty lines, it is said:[27]

> ...*pledge* because it is something that should not be breached;[28]
> *vow:* conviction about what you should and should not do.[29]

He thus describes [1] a practice that does not breach a promise and [2] stopping and restraining from not doing what should be done, and from doing what should not be done, respectively. [382] Since [Abhayākara, in his] *Vajrāvalī of Maṇḍala Rituals* and [Bhāvabhadra, in his] *Commentary on the Vajraḍāka Tantra* also explain pledge and vow in this way, this is how they should be understood.

Pledges of Ratnasaṃbhava

> In the great, excellent Jewel family always, three times day and night, give the four gifts—of materials, fearlessness, doctrine, and love. [Vś 767.4–5]

The "great Jewel" is Ratnasaṃbhava. In his "family always, three times day and night," in other words, six times, "give the four gifts—of materials" and so forth. The line "They say this is the vow pledge of the pure Jewel family" does not appear in the *Vajra Tip Tantra* nor in [Ānandagarbha's] *Illumination of the "Compendium of Principles"* and *Long*

Śrīparamādya Commentary. It is indicated by the first line ["In the great, excellent Jewel family"]. The same is true for the Action family.

Pledges of Amitābha

> You should keep the good Dharma—the external, secret, and the three vehicles. They say this is the pledge vow of the pure Lotus family. [Vś 767.5–6]

"You should keep the good Dharma" of "the three vehicles," and so forth.[30] "They say this is the pledge vow" of the completely "pure Lotus" Amitābha "family."

Pledges of Amoghasiddhi

> In the great, excellent, Action family, keep possession of all the vows perfectly, and as much as you are able, offer worship. [Vś 767.6–7]

It says, "in the Action" Amoghasiddhi "family keep all the vows perfectly, and...offer worship" as well.

General Pledges

This [383] has three parts: the root pledges, the branch pledges, and a summary.

Root Pledges

> Besides these, they explain fourteen defeats by opposition. Do not ignore and make light of them. They are said to be root downfalls. Recite them three times every day and three times at night. When yogis break them, gross immorality occurs. [Vś 767.7–768.1]

"Besides" the individual pledges of the five families, "do not ignore" mentally or "make light of" any of the shared pledges physically and verbally. What are these? First this indicates the root pledges, the "fourteen" commitments "mentioned" in the tantras [to avoid] "defeats by the opposition." They are also referred to by a second name, "root downfalls." When they occur, the vow is broken and the antidote is defeated. They are "defeats by the opposition" because the defeat is inflicted by the opposing side. A certain earlier writer glosses "ignoring" all the root downfalls and "not making light of" the antidotes.

What, then, are the fourteen root downfalls? I will set them out correctly and explain them in detail later [438ff]. An earlier practitioner of yoga says that transgressing the Three Jewels in the first family; the vajra, bell, and masters in the second; the four offerings in the third; the three doctrines in the fourth; and generosity alone in the last make up the fourteen.[31] Another person says the fourteen are the opposites of the five vows from not killing up to not drinking,[32] desisting from the two of being devoted to the holy ones and offering veneration to spiritual practitioners, the ten nonvirtues that compose wrong [384] physical actions—all of these together being counted as one, the four opposites of not pining for the Hīnayāna, and so forth,[33] thinking deities and so forth are unimportant, and walking over pictures of them and the like.

These two positions are wrong. Why? Because these [the actual fourteen shared vows in highest yoga tantra] explained in the *Vajra Tip Tantra* are not only proclaimed in yoga tantra, but are also vows spoken of in highest yoga tantra, [and while it might be possible to think that the vows given in the second position define a yoga tantra ordination, nobody could think that such a shared morality defines a highest yoga tantra ordination]. And [since the vows in highest yoga tantra are self-evidently intimately connected with the family buddha pledges], at such a time [when proclaiming the fourteen vows] it would not be right to interpret [the *Vajra Tip Tantra*'s] "Besides these the fourteen..." to refer to them.

The question may arise: does this [*Vajra Tip Tantra* proclamation of the fourteen root defeats] serve as the proclamation of vows in highest yoga tantra contexts as well? Yes it does. For Śāntipa in his *Commentary on [Dīpaṃkarabhadra's] Guhyasamāja Maṇḍala Ritual* and Jayabhadra in his nine-hundred-line *Saṃvara Maṇḍala Ritual*[34] proclaim the vows in the way that the *Vajra Tip Tantra* does, and say they are to be kept. And since the rituals described in the *Vajra Tip Tantra* are seen to be similar in terms of keeping vows, those proclamations of pledges to be kept are also shared in common. It seems, therefore, that in Indian maṇḍala rituals there are a number of different complete and incomplete presentations of the proclamation of the vows set out in the *Vajra Tip Tantra*.[35]

Now, you may say that the earlier [of the two wrong] positions is correct,[36] because [Ānandagarbha, in his] *Illumination of* (the first part of) *the "Compendium of Principles"* says:

> Tathāgata morality is defined as the opposite of the fourteen defeats by the opposition [indicated in the passage that] begins "Just like the lords of the three times, so shall I produce the unequalled... [Vś 768.7–769.6]"

And because he says in part 2 of the *Long Śrīparamādya Commentary* [385] in commenting on the lines, "Never forsake the vajra, bell, and mudrā..." [Vś 769.3]

> Just by the mere thought, these [defeats] happen. For [just by thinking] "There is no purpose in the mudrā and so forth," you give up the pledge completely and are defeated.

This does not seem to be correct. The meaning of the former quotation is as follows. Having taught that the vows of the five families indicated in the passage beginning, "Just like the lords..." is Tathāgata morality, insofar as morality is the opposite of wrongdoing, it teaches what it is in opposition to. It therefore says, "[Tathāgata morality is defined as] the opposite of the fourteen defeats by the opposition." Just saying that does not enable you to hold that a defeat [one of the fourteen root downfalls] is the opposite of a pledge of the five families. And even if [the passage in Vś 768.7–769.6] did enable you to hold that [view, that the opposites of the family pledges define the fourteen root downfalls], it should teach the opposite of the production of the thought of enlightenment as being a defeat [because not giving up bodhicitta is unquestionably one of the fourteen shared vows]. However, it does not in fact proclaim this [until later on in the next line]. Furthermore, the *Vajra Tip Tantra* says, "Besides these..." [implying a list of fourteen root downfalls that are different than the opposites of the family pledges].

Since the latter quotation explains forsaking a mudrā as a defeat, it harms [the first of the two wrong positions], because that [first position] does not mention [a mudrā] in the Vajra family [as does Ānandagarbha].

How, then, to understand the *Śrīparamādya Tantra* [on which Ānandagarbha's commentary is based, and based on which I will give the actual list of the fourteen vows]? It reads:

> All the buddhas agree that they should always guard this pledge vow siddhi. It is the word of the eternally good. They [practitioners] should not give up the bodhicitta that leaves no doubt about buddhahood just from its being produced (as the mudrā vajra). They should not disparage the holy doctrines and should never give them up. They should not disparage out of ignorance or unknowing. They should not reject their own selves and torture themselves with severe asceticism. They should joyfully relax, [386] [because] they are the complete buddha to come. They should never forsake the vajra, bell, and mudrā, and should not disparage the masters.

Among the pledges mentioned, forsaking three pledges [the vajra, bell, and mudrā] have been described as defeats in the above extract [cited 385.1]. Also, in his commentary on "not disparage the holy doctrines," [Ānandagarbha] says:

> Question: How should you understand the statement that they should not give up the doctrines of the three vehicles? [Response]: It is a defeat because the *Ākāśagarbha Sūtra* says, "If you reject the holy doctrine spoken in either the Listener, Pratyekabuddha, or Bodhisattva vehicles, your roots of virtue are destroyed, and you are defeated and [reborn in] Avīci hell, and so forth."

He thus establishes that giving up the doctrines of the three vehicles is a root downfall, as does Śāntipa. Therefore you should know that those remaining—giving up bodhicitta, hurting the aggregates, and disparaging the guru—are also root downfalls. These *Śrīparamādya Tantra* pledges are also mentioned in many texts, such as [Dīpaṃkarabhadra's] *Guhyasamāja Maṇḍala Ritual,* and are therefore rules that both share in common. In his *Introduction to the Meaning of the Tantras,* the master Buddhaguhya also uses these passages from the *Śrīparamādya Tantra* to substantiate his claim that pledges explained as common to all deities in other tantras are all brought together in the pledges of the *Compendium of Principles,* the *Vajra Tip Tantra,* and the *Śrīparamādya Tantra.* And [Munendrabhadra's] *Short Explanation of [Ānandagarbha's] "Maṇḍala Ritual Called Sarvavajrodaya"* [based on the] *Vajradhātumahāmaṇḍala* [of the *Compendium of Principles*] says [387] that you should guard against all the root downfalls explained in these passages of the *Śrīparamādya Tantra,* and the root downfalls explained elsewhere too. Therefore, this [yoga] commentary also supposes that the root downfalls of the two higher tantras are similar.

I have already explained the words "pledge" and "vow." When the siddhi of Vajrasattva and so forth is given, the "siddhi" is complete. Śāntipa explains "siddhi" as Amogha[siddhi], but it comes to the same thing. "They should always" in every instant "guard" and protect "this," the pledges that will be explained. "Say equally" means say it at one time with one voice. Through constant accomplishment, they should respectfully guard the pledges and vows that "the eternally," in the sense of definitively, "good," or excellent ones, that is, the tathāgatas, speak about when they say "you should not give up bodhicitta," and so forth.

"Bodhi" is full awakening to the knowledge of your own mind just as it is, and "citta" is what has that for its nature and is the cause of its attainment. There [are two types of bodhicitta:] prayer bodhicitta and the bodhicitta after setting out. Since they, "just from being produced, produce" the irreversible imprint "that leaves no doubt," you should have no doubt, given the sameness of the buddhas in the three periods of time, about the present buddhahood that the yogis understand [as their attainment]. So, "they should not give up" this [bodhicitta].

Question: How is it produced? It is produced "as the" five-pointed vajra "mudrā" that is the "vajra" of emptiness on a moon disk in the heart, having made a complete investigation [of its ultimate nature]. [388]

"They should not" ever, thinking that there is nothing in them, "disparage the doctrines" of the three vehicles taught by "holy" beings, or thinking, "There is nothing necessary in them, so I reject them," "give them up" either mentally or with words.

"They," the practitioners, "should not disparage" the doctrines, whether "through ignorance" when the wisdom that arises from study has not yet ascertained what the doctrines mean, or "through unknowing," when ignorant of the nature of dependent arising because of a lack of wisdom arisen from listening, thinking, and meditation. [Understand the "they" as students that the māntrikas teach, because Dīpaṃkarabhadra's] *Guhyasamāja Maṇḍala Ritual* says, "Whether out of unknowing or ignorance, do not reveal the great system," and [Ratnākaraśānti in his] *Commentary* to this says:

> When those without luck, or down on their luck, hear the words and meaning of the good doctrine, it leads to doubts or misconceptions, so do not teach them the meaning of the words.

Since the word "self" can refer to [the nature of] external things, to eliminate these [from consideration] it says both "their own" and "self." "They should not reject" or neglect their body and life, and "torture themselves" with the eighteen unbearable "severe asceticisms," and so forth, such as the severe dietary asceticism that composes the yogic remedies described in the action tantras. For the eighteen, read the *Trailokyavijaya Tantra Commentary.*

Question: How should they take [things]? [They should take it] "easy" without severe asceticism and extreme hardship. They should "enjoyably take" [things easy] and make their practice stronger with bedding, clothes, and sustenance that harmonizes with life, because "this"—there in the aggregates, definitely irreversible from enlightenment—"is the Buddha to come." Śāntipa says, [389] "They should not forsake the yogic mindset and torment themselves with what clashes with yoga."

The "vajra" is the hand symbol that has as its essence the first vajra that signifies bodhicitta. The "bell" is the bell marked by the first vajra, and is the hand symbol corresponding to the sound signifying wisdom. The "mudrās" are four: pledge, doctrine, action, and great mudrā. Śāntipa says that the way you reject them is to think, "You attain enlightenment by meditating on ultimate reality, so such things as a vajra and bell are of no use for attaining enlightenment." The *Long Śrīparamādya Commentary* cited earlier says that doing this is a root downfall, so be extremely careful because these are serious immoralities that are prone to happen.

To "disparage the masters" is to disparage them saying, "You are immoral," and so forth.

These pledges, found in many ritual texts, have to be made known to disciples, so I have clearly explained them as they are found in the *Long Śrīparamādya Commentary.*

Question: If the two systems taught above do not explain the meaning of [the *Vajra Tip Tantra* statement], "Besides these the fourteen defeats...," what does it mean?

[Response]: The *Vajra Tip Tantra* does indeed say there are fourteen root downfalls set forth in yoga tantra. But there does not seem to be any other authoritative Indian [yoga tantra] text that explains just what the fourteen are. [Munendrabhadra's] *Short Explanation of* [Ānandagarbha's] *"Maṇḍala Ritual Called Sarvavajrodaya"* [based on the] *Vajradhātu Mahāmaṇḍala* [of the *Compendium of Principles*], as mentioned above, does talk [about fourteen vows]. Also, the *vajrācārya* Kāmadhenu of Jalaṇdhara[37] in his *Commentary* on the *Cleansing All States of Woe Tantra* [390] sets out the ritual for taking the special vows shared in common in the section beginning, "Therefore always..." up to, "The ultimate reality of oneself and similarly of the mantra, and so forth," and then he says, "Give to those suitable to be a master [the knowledge of] the fourteen root and branch downfalls." Then he goes on, when announcing the pledges, to say:

> "In regard to those real vajra women..." in regard to those real yoginīs who are not differentiable, as vajra-wisdom, from Bhagavatī, Cundā, Ekajaṭī, Māmakī, and Tārā, and so forth. "Yoga practitioners," or tantric practitioners, "should not consider low," or should stop disparaging them, based on their being women. [The *Vajra Vehicle Root Downfalls*] says:[38] "The fourteenth is despising women whose essence is wisdom." Thus it also sets forth holding them inferior as a root downfall.

Thus he says the root downfall of disparaging women is a root downfall in yoga tantra, and he clearly accepts that the other thirteen are similar to [downfalls] as well. And this is quite correct because [1] the fourteen downfalls define the rules of those who are keeping the five family vows, [2] the explanations of the ritual for taking the vows of the five families are the same in the *Vajra Tip Tantra*, the *Saṃpuṭa Tantra*,[39] and the *Ḍākārṇava Yoginī Tantra*,[40] and especially because [3] the proclamation of the fourteen downfalls when the vows are proclaimed is common [to both]. Hence, although some differences do occur among the downfalls based on the fact that there is a graduated difference [between yoga and highest yoga] tantra, you should harmonize the general list of names and the general nature of the vows with the scriptures in which the fourteen root downfalls are found. And if there are, in fact, fourteen downfalls [in yoga tantra] quite different from those in highest yoga tantra, why didn't scholars [391] such as the three masters of yoga tantra [Ānandagarbha, Buddhaguhya, and Śākyamitra] at least list the names [of such vows] clearly? [They should have done so if they existed,] because generally you engage [in good] and avoid [wrong] after coming to understand the pledges and vows. In particular, after identifying the root downfalls you guard against them—a practice that is indispensable for everyone in the beginning. The master Buddhaguhya in his *Introduction to the Meaning of the Tantras* says:

> Then those who have pleased the gurus are taught the collection of Mahāyāna realization by them: the great maṇḍalas, the pledges, doctrines, and proper ritual consecration in the action maṇḍalas. Knowledgeable about keeping vows as they are found in the rituals, the pledges which are to be kept, the Vinaya, and proper behavior and its range, from then on, in order to protect the pledges [and keep them] as they were when they [first] arose, their enthusiasm should never decline, because these are the first prerequisites for accomplishing their own and others' aims.

Therefore, those of you who are wise: Definitely accept the fourteen root downfalls of yoga tantra like this! [As to what exactly constitutes each downfall], I will teach that below.

[Returning, now, to the remaining lines from VŚ 767.7–768.1] "Recite them" and examine whether your mind is or is not stained by a fault "three times every day and three times in the night," three times day and night. "When" they "break" or violate "them," meaning the pledges to be gone through and inspected, "yogis" incur an "immorality," a "gross" downfall.

The root pledges are simply an example. You have to do the same [i.e., go through them and see if they have been broken] with all the root and branch pledges as well, [392] because Saraha says in his *Buddha Kapāla Maṇḍala Ritual:*

> Those pure in mind get up early, and while eating protect their vows. They protect the vows and pledges without regard to body

> and life. Three times by day and three times by night they should always recite them. When yogis break them, gross immorality occurs.

Similarly, Lawapa in his *Saṃvara Maṇḍala Ritual* and Nagpopa in his *Saṃvara Maṇḍala Ritual* also mention protecting while eating as a general pledge [and a means of continually bringing the pledges to mind day and night]. So, you who are new to the work! Divide up each twenty-four hours into six periods and be mindful. The investigation of whether or not faults have occurred at these times is an incomparable method for protecting your pledges.

Branch Pledges

This has three parts: teaching negatively framed pledges, positively framed pledges, and additional negatively framed pledges.

Negatively Framed Pledges

> You should not kill the living, take what is not given, or engage in perverted pleasures. And you should not tell a lie. Give up that root of all ruination, alcoholic beverages. Except to tame living beings, give up everything that should not be done. [Vś 768.1–3]

On top of the four things to give up—from killing to lying—there is the giving up of drinking alcohol. These are the five foundations for practice. It is necessary to protect them as the foundation for accomplishments. The *Vajra Tip Tantra* says:

> If you want the supreme siddhi, having gone to the Three Jewels for refuge, [393] keep at the five trainings and work supremely hard at bodhicitta. [Vś 852.1–2]

The statement that drinking alcohol is the "root of all ruination," that is, faults, is not only applicable to yoga tantra, but common to highest yoga tantras as well, because many authentic maṇḍala rituals explain this just as the *Vajra Tip Tantra* does. All wrong conduct "that should not be done" by body, speech, and mind should be given up "except" in the case of some bodhisattvas who keep the vows of the supreme vehicle correctly and have firm bodhicitta. As explained in *Great Vairocana's Enlightenment Discourse,* there are occasions when, "to train living beings," they do the seven [normally nonvirtuous actions] of body and speech, such as killing and so forth.

Positively Framed Pledges

> You should devote yourself to holy persons and serve practitioners. And to the extent of your abilities, you should cultivate the three physical actions, the four actions of speech, and the three actions of mind. [Vś768.3–4]

You should "devote yourself to holy" friends and achieve a knowledge of mantra. For as it says in the *Vajra Tip Tantra* [684.7–685.1], "To achieve a knowledge of mantra, practitioners should devote themselves to the wise."

You should also not disparage "practitioners" but should "serve" them. And to the extent you are able, "you should cultivate" and increase the ten actions of the three doors [of body, speech, and mind].

Additional Negatively Framed Pledges

This has two parts: avoiding the cause for reversing from the Mahāyāna and avoiding the fault of disparaging and walking on top [of holy objects].

Avoiding the Cause of Reversing from the Mahāyāna

> You should not crave the Deficient Vehicle. You should not turn your back [394] on the needs of living beings. You should not reject cyclic existences. You should never be attached to nirvāṇa. [Vś 758.4–5]

The "Deficient Vehicle" refers to the śrāvaka and pratyekabuddha paths, deficient because its aim is not the needs of others and its result is not enlightenment. "You should not crave" a course for yourself by way of that path. I have already explained how thinking, "As far as I am concerned the Deficient Vehicle scriptures are useless," is wrong. Do not, on account of defeatism and so forth, "turn your back on" or develop dislike for the burdensome commitment of looking after the needs of infinite numbers of living beings. Take on the burden with enthusiasm. As for not rejecting "cyclic existence," the *Vajra Tip Tantra* [694.5] says:

> May I not become a buddha until the very end of cyclic existence. And may I similarly work to establish all living beings in that state.

Thus you put on armor for the sake of living beings and remain in cyclic existence until the stream of existence ends.

"Never" at any time "be attached to" the attainment of "nirvāṇa," or mere freedom from the bonds of existence. Rather, strive for complete enlightenment.

Avoiding the Fault of Disparaging and Walking on Holy Objects

You should not disparage the gods, the opponents of the gods, or lesser spirits. You should not step over their mudrā, conveyances, weapons, or what symbolizes them. [Vś 768.5]

"You should not disparage the gods or the opponents of the gods," be they extraordinary or ordinary, "or lesser spirits" such as *yakṣas* and so forth. Jayabhadra also has the reading [in his *Saṃvara Maṇḍala Ritual*], "You should not disparage the three *guhyaka* gods."

A "mudrā" [in this instance] is a drawing of a god's body, and so forth. [395] A "conveyance" of a god is something that has been fashioned into a conveyance for a god and the conveyance of a guru. A "weapon" is a divine hand symbol such as a sword, and so on. "What symbolizes them" is the divine hand symbol such as the wheel, the vajra, and so forth. These should not be stepped over. The *Vajra Tip Tantra* [685.3–5]:

> You should not step over, nor should you eat [replicas of] any symbolic mudrā such as the wheel, vajra, bell, and so forth. Similarly, you should not tread on leftovers or a god's shadow, nor should you sit on them. You should not set them out again. You should not step over and disparage a god's auspicious hand symbol or symbols of the conveyances of gods. You should not hurt living beings.

And [Vś 823.1–3]:

> You should not walk over a god's body or hand symbol, the conveyances of gods, leftovers, or the shadow of a god or anything that symbolizes a god, and you should not eat edibles that have been fashioned into symbolic representations. Edibles that have been fashioned into symbolic representations should never be trod on.

"Leftovers" are old things that have already been offered. You should not sit on these or put something else on top of them, and so forth.

The *Introduction to the Meaning of the Tantras* clearly explains what is to be done when walking on shadows and so on is unavoidable:

> An exception to the rule has been made for those with the vajra force and for mahāmudrā practitioners when, through the force of place and time, they walk over and tread on what should not be walked over, and so forth. When through the force of place and time these two do so, still those practitioners do not incur the fault of walking over what is not to be walked over and so forth. [396]

As others say:

> Your pledges will definitely be broken if, through ignorance and stupidity, or through laziness and forgetfulness, you tread on a vajra picture and so on. Therefore, with a total effort, with the vajra force, those who are wise know how not to stray, particularly when going into a maṇḍala. There is no fault, when you have the vajra force, even if leftovers, pictures of vajras, symbolic representations, and the assembly of buddhas and consorts are below and if you tread on them.

They say the same about mudrā yoga as well, because they specify it with the statement "in place of the words 'the vajra force' put the words 'mudrā yoga.'" They then teach the vajra force mudrā and the tantric yoga as follows, "Your pledges do not get broken when you enter into and emerge from pictorial or vajra figurative representations [of maṇḍalas] after having mentally raised them up."

Though they say *vajra pictures* and *vajra figurative representations,* these are only examples. Notice that included as well are other things that should not be walked over, such as mudrās and so forth. That is the mental mudrā. The mantra that goes with it is *vajra vegākrama.*

The second part of the *Compendium of Principles* says:

> The heart of the vajra force is: *Oṃ vajra vegākrama hūṃ.* In that fashion go where you will, crossing the pictures of all maṇḍalas, even the Dharmadhātu maṇḍala and so forth. [397]

Next is the explanation of the heart of that. Having mentally raised up the picture, be it a vajra figurative representation or whatever, later when you have entered in, you will not have violated your pledge.

Ānandagarbha [in his *Illumination of the "Compendium of Principles"*] explains "picture" as a picture [of a maṇḍala] drawn with colors, and "figurative representation" as a picture made with strings of the five colors. He explains "raising up" as mentally visualizing slipping in under them. Since it says "or whatever," these are merely examples. Hence you should say the mantra verbally like that, while mentally visualizing the location you are crossing as being on top of you, and slipping in under the place.

Since it talks even about how those scared to break their pledges in ways like this avoid faults, you have to work hard to protect against even the tiniest wrongdoing. As it says in the *Vajra Tip Tantra* [826.7]:

> Then take the commitments specific to the knowledge woman and do not give up your vows. To have engaged in even a speck of immorality is a reason to feel regret.

Summary of the Explanation of the General Pledges

> These are said to be the pledges. You should always keep them. [Vś 768.5–6]

Connect "these" with everything from the proclamation of general pledges explained above on down, because the meaning of these two sentences is present in the individual pledges of the five families [and does not need to be spelled out].

> The secret tantras explain at length the vows in agreement with these. [Vś 768.6]

It then says explicitly that all the "tantras explain at length the vows," or the places where one is to train, that are "in agreement with these," the aforementioned ones, in order to eliminate the notion that perhaps these are all there are.

Having proclaimed these pledges to be taken in order to make them known, with the intention [398] to keep them, you take them by way of the ritual that I will explain below. In a word, when you take the vows, you take them within their being clearly delineated—not half-knowing, and half-not knowing them.

There are also some maṇḍala rituals in which no part of the text proclaims the vows. Here also, the master gives a rough outline of the vows to be taken, and after making sure the disciples are clear about them, causes them to be taken.

I have constructed this out of those parts of the text of the *Vajra Tip Tantra* in which the proclamation of the vows is found.

2. Taking Tantric Vows

THERE IS A RITUAL for taking the vows in the fourth section of the third part of the *Saṃpuṭa Tantra,* the twelfth section of the *Ḍākārṇava Yoginī Tantra,* and in the Vajra Master section of the *Vajra Tip Tantra.* Here the explanation is based on the text of the *Vajra Tip Tantra.* It has two parts: requesting ordination and taking vows.

Requesting Ordination

In the *Vajra Tip Tantra,* disciples who request ordination begin by saying:

> Sage, Sun, Fully Enlightened Being, please turn your thoughts to me, please grant me ordination... [Vś 766.1–7]

Then they are asked if from the bottom of their heart they wish to take the ordination, or if they do not, as follows:

> Do you wish, noble one, to keep the secret of those in the great secret family? [Vś 766.7–767.1]

If the disciple has a yearning, first the master announces the vows and then the disciples request with:

> Master, please listen to my request. [Vś 768.6]

The ordination is then given. In the *Vajra Tip Tantra* [851.6–852.1] it also says:

> The wise should give these vows to them [399] based on how much they want and admire them. They should not give them under duress. If they have faith, the ordination should be given.

> Having established them in the three vows, the maṇḍala should then be taught.

This lets it be known that the vows should not be given to disciples who do not want to take them, but only to those who have faith and who want to take them. And, as just explained, it is necessary to inquire about, and find out if from the bottom of their hearts they wish to take the ordination or if they do not. It is important that this be not just a passing fancy to receive a consecration, and that the master causes a heartfelt wish to take the ordination to arise, because if this is absent, the ordination will not occur.

Even if disciples want to take the ordination, it still will not occur if the master has broken his earlier tantric vows by incurring a root downfall. Hence, in giving the qualifications of a vajra master, the *Vajra Tent Tantra,* the *Saṃvarodaya Tantra,* and so forth say that he should not have a root downfall. And Mañjuśrīkīrti in his *Ornament for the Essence* says:

> Distance yourself from vajra masters who are not keeping the three vows, who keep on with a root downfall, who are miserly with the Dharma, and who engage in actions that should be forsaken. Those who worship them go to hell and so on as a result.

You might wonder, in that case, if there is anyone with a supreme vehicle ordination—since the Vajra Vehicle root downfalls seem so many and so quick to occur, since the time of the degeneration of the doctrine is at hand, and, since when it comes to the two higher [sets of tantra], it is extremely rare to see [400] someone who has understood even a line of advice about the root [vows], never mind someone who is keeping them. This is not a problem. Masters who are going to give disciples consecration initially have entry into the maṇḍala as their own practice, and receive consecration, pledges, and vows. Hence, at that time, they are motivated by the wish to take the pledges and vows and do so in accord with the rites. They produce the ordination again even if it has been broken earlier. Thus, the master giving the consecration comes to have the vows. So you should understand that this is the reason that it is said that masters themselves should enter the maṇḍala before giving empowerment. As Śākyamitra says in his *Commentary on the "Compendium of Principles," Ornament of Kosala:*

> When it is time to grant entrance to a disciple, first the master should undergo the rites of entrance. This is because it is possible that some have transgressed certain pledges through forgetfulness. Hence, masters should first of all enter themselves.

In the *Ḍākārṇava Tantra* the request is, "All buddhas and bodhisattvas, please turn your thoughts to me." The *Saṃpuṭa Tantra* is similar. Here is what it means. "Buddhas" are those who are fully enlightened. [Construe] "bodhisattvas" as follows: "bodhi" is the assembly of the gods [in a maṇḍala]. Those adepts who know those to be their own minds *[sattva]* and whose minds are in the form of the deities are bodhisattvas. Bhāvabhadra [in his *Commentary on the Vajraḍāka Tantra*] says: "Please turn your thoughts" is a joyful request saying, "Please bestow blessing and take me as your own."

Taking the Vows

The *Vajra Tip Tantra* [768.7] summarizes the commitment with:

> Leader, [401] I shall strive to do just as you say.

This has three parts: production of the thought, actual ordination, and summarizing the commitment.

Production of the Thought

> Just like the lords during the three periods of time were set on enlightenment, so too shall I produce the unequalled and supreme bodhicitta. [Vś 768.7–769.1]

"During the three periods of time"—the past, present, and future—when they were bodhisattvas, "the lords," the protectors of living beings, the buddhas who have gone, are going, and will go to enlightenment, "were set on" or were one-pointedly focused on "enlightenment"—the completion of personal welfare and the welfare of others. "Just like" they, for example, produced, are producing, and will produce bodhicitta encompassing all the equipment of generosity, and so forth that is for enlightenment, "so too shall I produce" it.

Both Bhāvabhadra and Abhayākara [in his *Clusters of Quintessential Instructions*] understand that the thought of enlightenment that has to be produced must be both the thought of enlightenment that is a prayer and the thought of enlightenment after having set out. In this context you do not get the thought of enlightenment after having set out [just] by taking bodhisattva ordination. That [bodhisattva ordination] is only a [necessary] part of taking tantric ordination. This is similar to [Śāntideva's] mention of the thought of enlightenment that is a prayer in his *Engaging in the Bodhisattva Deeds* in the context of the ritual for taking vows of the thought of enlightenment after having set out [that define, in the general, nontantric context, a person who has set out for enlightenment].

In the *Ḍākārṇava Tantra* (and similarly in the *Long Śrīparamādya Tantra Commentary*) the translation reads:

> ...being set on perfect enlightenment [by earlier bodhisattvas], so too the thought of unsurpassed enlightenment [by me today]...

This is better because it needs to be [syntactically] connected with the "so too." Here the prayer is a yearning prayer that I, [402] myself, will become Vajrasattva and will set all living beings into that state. Having set out is to be practicing that [Vajrasattva's] path of giving and so forth. This is Bhāvabhadra's idea. And since both accomplish an unequalled result, they are "unequalled" and "supreme."

Before this passage [beginning "Just like the lords..."] the *Ḍākārṇava Tantra* and similarly the *Saṃpuṭa Tantra* say, "I who am called so-and-so, from this time, right up until I get to the terrace of enlightenment," giving the name of whoever is producing bodhicitta and the length of time for which it is being produced. "Enlightenment" is non-abiding nirvāṇa; "terrace" is the supreme [place] of the enlightenment [of all buddhas]; "get to" is reach. Where it says, "I who am called so-and-so," you give your own name, the idea being that you really are committing yourself. "From" means starting with; "this time" refers to a point in time. Alternatively, following Bhāvabhadra's explanation, take "from" to mean starting from when the blessings of the buddhas gave the impetus. You should know that in the earlier [passage VŚ 766.1–7] too, as Abhayākara says, you say your name so that you will not go back on the promise you made.

The Actual Ordination

This has five parts: taking the vows of Vairocana, Akṣobhya, Ratnasaṃbhava, Amitābha, and Amoghasiddhi.

Taking Vairocana's Vows

> In the Buddha-yoga vows are the three moralities: the training in morality, the morality that brings together wholesome dharmas, and the morality of working for the welfare of living beings. I will keep them firmly. From today on I will keep [403] the unsurpassed Three Jewels of Buddha, Dharma, and Community [as refuge]. [Vś 769.1–3]

Here the *Ḍākārṇava Tantra* says:

> The Buddha-yoga product vows are, from today on, to keep the Buddha, Dharma, and Community—the unsurpassed Three Jewels—as supreme [refuge]. I will firmly keep each of the three moralities: the training in morality, the morality that brings together wholesome dharmas, and the morality of working for the welfare of living beings.

Thus it also says that keeping the three moralities is a vow of Vairocana. Bhāvabhadra says this as well. Abhayākara does not say so clearly, but the former [position] is best, since both the *Vajra Tip Tantra* and *Ḍākārṇava Tantra* say [that keeping the three moralities] is a vow of Vairocana, and the *Long Śrīparamādya Commentary*, the *Maṇḍala Ritual Called Sarva-vajrodaya*, Nagpochopa's *Mahāmāyā Maṇḍala Ritual*, and Jayabhadra's *Saṃvara Maṇḍala Ritual* and so forth have a passage similar to the one in the *Vajra Tip Tantra*. However, the translation in the *Ḍākārṇava Tantra* is better. Section twelve of the *Ornament of the Vajra Essence Tantra* says that production of bodhicitta alone is the Tathāgata family pledge.

But why, when proclaiming the vows, does it only mention taking refuge in the Three Jewels as a vow of Vairocana? This is not a slip. This is similar to what happens during the proclamation of the vows—the common pledges are mentioned then, even though they are not mentioned during the ordination [proper]. [404] Since the thought of enlightenment after having set out was generated earlier [in the consecration ritual, where the candidate for tantra takes bodhisattva ordination], it is not correct, as some other texts would have it,[41] to connect the practice of the three moralities with taking the vows relating to the thought of enlightenment after having set out [that define, in the tantric context, a person who has set out for enlightenment]. Hence the master Munendrabhadra is wrong when he says [1] that you produce prayer bodhicitta with the lines [Vś 768.7–769.1] "Just like the lords during the three periods of time"; [2] that a bodhisattva who is practicing at the door of tantra takes vows shared with the Perfection [Vehicle] with the lines [Vś 769.1–2] "In the Buddha-yoga vows are the three moralities"; and [3] then takes unique [tantric] bodhisattva vows with the lines [Vś 769.2–3] "From today on I will take [refuge in] the unsurpassed Three Jewels."

Here [Abhayākara in his] *Ornament of the Sage's Thought* says:

> The production of bodhicitta is the vow of the three moralities,
> and just that with a special feature is the consecration vow.

Thus he says the tantric vow is the vow of the three moralities with a "special feature." And in his *Vajrāvalī of Maṇḍala Rituals* he says the special feature is in the systemization of the five families, hence the vows of the five families. So even though you have to connect the vow of the three moralities with the pledges of the other families as well, it is mentioned as the pledge of the Vairocana family, keeping in mind that this is the main one for him.

Now I shall explain what the text [following the *Ḍākārṇava Tantra* translation] means. "To keep" is the point of departure for the explanation. How long do you keep them and for what purpose? The earlier [citation from the *Ḍākārṇava Tantra* stating] "...up until I get to the terrace of enlightenment..." taught the first, [and the lines from the summarizing commitment] "...for the sake of all living beings..." teaches the second, [as explained] below. Keep what? "Buddha" is Vairocana; "product" is something born—the adept doing the "yoga" of this family; "vows/restraints" in the sense of what stop and encompass that [adept's] physical, verbal, and mental deeds that should not be done. [405] "Buddha" is one who has fully comprehended ultimate reality and eliminated both the obscurations and their residual impressions, that is, Vairocana and so forth. "Dharma" is in the sense of what holds, that is, the scriptures and the realization [of the scriptures]; they are "Community" in that they are collected together, such as Mañjuśrī and so forth. These are the *Konchog Sum,* [the Tibetan rendering of] the "Three Jewels." *Chog* means "supreme" among all that is *kon* or "rare," hence, "unsurpassed." They [the vows/restraints] are to go for refuge, and so forth to those [objects]. How long do you keep [the refuge]? "From today on" until the terrace of enlightenment. How do you keep [the refuge]? As "supreme," the most important thing. "Keep" means to cause them to be produced, in the sense of first going for refuge, and afterward making them manifest.

And also "keep." Keep what? "The three moralities." Which three? "Training" vows, which are "the morality" that turns back from the unwholesome, "the morality that brings together wholesome dharmas," embracing the wholesome, and "the morality of working for the welfare of living beings," which does what others need. [Abhayākara] in his *Clusters of Quintessential Instructions* says that the first settles the mind, the second causes the Buddhadharmas to ripen in your own mindstream, and the third ripens the mindstreams of others. This is what [Asaṅga] intends in the *Bodhisattva Levels.* The *Clusters of Quintessential Instructions* construes [the dual compound] "brings together the wholesome and the dharmas" [in place of the adjectival compound "brings together wholesome dharmas"] and says "the wholesome" is the vow of morality that separates you from the unwholesome.

Who keeps them? "I will..." They produce a heroic intent, because it will say [in the summarizing commitment], "To free all wandering beings, commit yourself with pride." How do they keep them? "Firmly," not falling back through the power of ignorance from the bodhicitta and so forth to which they are committed, and "each," taking them over and over. Connect "firmly keep each" with all the following [vows] as well. [406]

The *Long Śrīparamādya Commentary* reads "In the Buddha yoga, vows are vow morality..." The *Saṃpuṭa Tantra* and so forth has "...the Buddha yoga..." and so on in a later position, preceded by the passage about keeping the three moralities. You should know that the meaning of these is the same.

Taking Akṣobhya's Vows

> Those in the great, supreme Vajra family shall properly keep the vajra, bell, and mudrā [vows]. They shall also keep the master's [vow]. [Vś 769.3–4]

"Keep" refers to keeping what? "Also" means as well as the earlier vows, keep the "vajra" pledge, the "bell" pledge, and the "mudrā" pledge, and not only these, but also the "master's" pledge. Who pledges to keep them? Where the *Ḍākārṇava Tantra* says, "Those in the great, high Vajra family..." it is explained that "high Vajra" means Akṣobhya, and "those in the family" are the adepts connected with him. Hence, they are their pledges. Or it is explained that the vows or restraints themselves are the great, high Vajra family because they are what Akṣobhya essentially is. Abhayākara reads, "The great Vajra family gathering..." and says "great Vajra" is Akṣobhya, and "family" the collection of gods emanating from him—that is, they are a "gathering" of Akṣobhya.

How do they keep them? They should keep them "properly," over and over again. And since the *Saṃpuṭa Tantra* says, "Keep each through [keeping in mind] what they really are," they should keep the vajra and so forth by way of [keeping in mind] what they really are. [407] How do they keep them by way of [keeping in mind] what they really are? As it says in the thirty-first section of the *Ḍākārṇava Tantra,* authentically keeping a vajra and bell is keeping a symbolic vajra and bell, and, knowing the meaning they symbolize, holding the vajra and ringing the bell. This is keeping [them] by [keeping in mind] what they really are.

Now, the nondual mind—the bodhicitta of all tathāgatas—is the secret or inner vajra. Keeping the external vajra, within recollecting that [inner vajra], is keeping the vajra by [keeping in mind] what it really is. Thus the second part of the *Long Śrīparamādya Tantra Commentary,* after the explanation of the meaning of the secret vajra as above, also says:

> Having brought this meaning of vajra clearly to mind, the Tathāgata family yogis should, picking up the Tathāgata vajra, keep [the vow]. In this way they keep the Tathāgata vajra by [keeping in mind] what it really is.

The Tathāgata yogis and Tathāgata vajra are examples [that apply to] the other families. The second part of the *Long Śrīparamādya Commentary* also says:

> Everything has space as its mark and space has no mark. Those whose yoga is comparable to space light up the supreme thing that is comparable in all.

Thinking that statements like this are resonating from the bell, as they ring the bell, they should believe in these words.

Just as space, the mere negation of all obstructing matter, is not an entity with an own-being, similarly everything is without own-being because it is, ultimately, from its very start, unproduced. Suchness is comparable to, or like, space. Those uniting[42] with that are yogis.[43] Their minds and mental factors are one taste with true reality. The transcendental wisdom of those yogis therefore lights up or encompasses suchness, which is the supreme thing that is comparable in all. As [in VŚ 767.3], "They say...wisdom is [408] the bell," such wisdom is what the bell symbolizes, and even though one rings a symbolic bell, ringing it with the idea that one is sounding out statements like those is keeping [the bell pledge] by [keeping in mind] what it really is.

They keep the mudrā [vow by keeping in mind] what it really is when, as yogis in one or the other family, they arise in the form of Vairocana and so forth, purify [i.e., symbolically transform] their state as an [ordinary] living being,[44] and recite mantra in meditation. The *Long Śrīparamādya Commentary* says:

> The Tathāgata yogis who want to accomplish the great mudrā of their Tathāgata should properly take hold of the vajra and ring the bell, [keeping in mind] what they really are. Then, having tightened the great mudrā of their Tathāgata, they should purify whatever the forms through which they will tame living beings. Then, thinking themselves to be, so to speak, the Tathāgata who has completed the work to be done, they should recite mantra or meditate.

Here the Tathāgata is just an example [for the other families]. The *Śrīparamādya Tantra* says:

> Hold the vajra [keeping in mind] what it really is, and ring the Dharma bell. Controlled by the great mudrā pledge, recite the heart [mantra].

What this means has been conveyed in the above [sections proclaiming the pledges], as well as in the section on bestowing the three [409] pledges.

Since these are three pledges common to both [yoga tantra and highest yoga tantra], you should not formulate the mudrā pledge only in terms of the mutual embrace of man and woman. The tightening of the mudrā should also be understood in a similar fashion, contextually.

Although the commentaries say you can take "master" to mean your guru and you can take it to mean [the person who gives] the master consecration, the former accords with the proclamation of the vow. The *Clusters of Quintessential Instructions* says that the way these [Tathāgata practitioners] keep the vow is by maintaining that [the master] causes the dawning of the transcendental understanding of the way things are—that is to say, they view [the master] as the sacred origin of siddhis.

Taking Ratnasaṃbhava's Vows

> For the pledge of the beautiful, great Jewel family, six times each day give the four sorts of gift—of materials, fearlessness, doctrine, and love. [Vś 769.4–5]

It says they "give." What? "The four sorts of gift." These are material things, doctrine, fearlessness, and love. Alternatively, they are wealth such as gold, essential or primary wealth such as grain and servants, a limb such as a foot, and an essential or primary limb such as the head, leg, and so forth. The *Clusters of Quintessential Instructions* has "pleasant words" in place of "love," and has the same latter four gifts except that it calls them wealth, limb, crucial wealth, and crucial limb. Who pledges such gifts? The Ratnasaṃbhava family siddhas who do the yoga connecting to that form with a single-pointed mind again and again. "Jewel" is transcendental understanding of sameness; [410] "family" is possessing the Jewel as its origin since it originates from that; "pledge" is what they are committed to not transgressing. Since those who like giving connect with that [Ratnasambhava], it is "beautiful" because they give pleasure. [My explanation here is based on] the translation, "Those with the pledges of the beautiful, great Jewel family yoga..." found in the *Ḍākārṇava Tantra,* and also in the *Saṃpuṭa Tantra.* The *Clusters of Quintessential Instructions* interprets the yoga to mean that with the gifts of Ratnasaṃbhava they give pleasure to living beings. The way they give is "six times"—

three times during the day and three times during the night. And as [Buddhaguhya in his] *Introduction to the Meaning of the Tantras* says, they must do it on a daily basis:

> Do not let the idea that you do not have many things to give away serve as a hindrance to daily giving. It is not important whether it is small or not very good, give what you can.[45] Never transgress because of that.

The [intensifying prefix] *pra-* [in "*pra-dā,*" "to give"] occurs in both [the *Ḍākārṇava* and *Saṃpuṭa*] *Tantras* as well.

Why, during the proclamation and taking of vows, does it only give the number of times each day for Ratnasaṃbhava's pledges, and not for the others? This is not a reference to the self-examination explained above [Vś 767.7–768.1], in which you examine six times to see whether or not you are stained with a root or branch pledge infraction. It is saying to give six times a day. This statement that you should observe your Ratnasaṃbhava pledge six times seems to serve as an instance for the other pledges as well, because the *Vajra Tip Tantra* [703.2–4] says:

> Take the vows in the morning and the same ones at noon and in the transition period. Three times in the day and night do the four sorts of Buddha, Vajra, Jewel, and Lotus [family] yoga, the Buddha, Dharma, and Community, [411] and enlightenment six times day and night; and the vajra, bell, feast master, and vajra-possessor six times as well.

"Buddha, Dharma, and Community" is refuge; "enlightenment" is the production of bodhicitta; "vajra-possessor" is the mudrā pledge. Do these "six" times—three times in the day and three times in the night. It needs to be investigated whether here, as elsewhere, there is no mention of the [Amoghasiddhi] action family, because [the text] speaks of four [families instead of five], incorporating the action family into the Jewel family. In any case do not construe it to mean the pledges of other families six times, but not his.

In expanding on the above lines the *Vajra Tip Tantra* [703.4–5] says:

> You should give material things, fearlessness, doctrine, and loving kindness each day as well. You should recite the three doctrines and the so-called four *brahmās* eightfold.[46]

What does this mean? [In response we say] the statement about four gifts six times was from the standpoint of time, not from the standpoint of internal divisions. This is because it makes [the statement that] the four [gifts have to be given] each time. It says "eight" referring to the internal division into four daily and four nightly gifts. "The three doctrines" are probably outer doctrines, secret doctrines, and the doctrine of the three vehicles spoken of in the context of the pledges of Amitābha, though this should be investigated. The former two [outer and secret] are combined into one and termed *secret mantra doctrine,* so that in keeping to the doctrine each day and night, by a process of internal division into four [secret mantra, srāvaka, pratyekabuddha, and bodhisattva] there are eight. Perhaps (but again this will have to be checked) the "four *brahmās*" are the four immeasurables [love, compassion, joy, and dispassion], well known as four grounds of the spiritual,[47] [and understood] as the accomplishing wisdom [of] Amoghasiddhi,[48] since the four immeasurables are the best method to accomplish work to be done for the sake of living beings. [412] You meditate on them day and night, and by internal division [they are eightfold].

Of the four sorts of gift, two—material things and doctrine—are straightforward. Understand the latter two, [fearlessness and love, as they are spoken of in] the *Vajra Tip Tantra:*

> Tolerant toward enemies, friends, and strangers, give fearlessness. Speaking gently and truthfully, meditate on love that overcomes hate.

The way to give gifts daily when you are not actually able to give material things or doctrine is by training in the idea of giving away your body and possessions to others, and in the idea of turning over wholesome dharmas [that you have cultivated] to others, since increasing the mental capacity to be positive after giving[49] is itself the primary training in giving. Also, having cultivated patience and love, give fearlessness and love. Similarly, with holding and worshipping doctrine, you actually [teach and worship] doctrine and mentally practice [the meaning that is conveyed]. The other two families are easy to understand.

Taking Amitābha's Vows

> Those in the pure, great Lotus family that comes from great enlightenment should keep the good Dharma—the external, secret, [and the] three vehicles.[50] [Vś 769.5]

They "should keep." Keep what? The "good" Buddha's "Dharma." The *Clusters of Quintessential Instructions* says (and Bhāvabhadra is of the same opinion) that "external" [Dharma] is the action tantras, such as the *Three Pledges Array Tantra* and the *Bhūtaḍāmara Tantra,* and the performance tantras such as *Great Vairocana's Enlightenment Discourse,* in which there are instructions on ritual actions such as bathing and purification and so forth, on external constructions, and on focusing on drawings of a deity's body and so on. "Secret" [413] [Dharma] is threefold: the yoga tantras such as the *Compendium of Principles,* the mahāyoga tantras such as the *Guhyasamāja Tantra,* and the highest yoga tantras such as the yoginī tantras. The "three vehicles" [Dharma] are the Śrāvaka and Pratyekabuddha [Vehicles] together with the Perfection [nontantric Mahāyāna] Definitions Vehicle,[51] because it talks about tantric Mahāyāna in terms of external and secret.

Munendrabhadra criticizes the assertion that "external" [Dharma] is the two Śrāvaka and Pratyekabuddha Vehicles together with the Perfections Mahāyāna as the third, and that the "secret" vehicles are the action, performance, and yoga vehicles. He says Buddhists[52] share the same objects of refuge, and that you posit [a doctrine] as internal or external in terms of whether it asserts or does not assert the four [basic tenets that seal a doctrine as authentically Buddhist]—all created things are impermanent, [all dharmas with outflows are suffering, all dharmas are empty, and nirvāṇa is peace]. Hence [he says] it is not proper to take Śrāvaka and Pratyekabuddha [Dharma] as "external." His position is that "external" Dharma is the *Vedas* and so forth, and the "secret" vehicles are the three of the Śrāvaka, Pratyekabuddha, and Mahāyāna. He reads [the compound "external-secret-vehicle-three" as "the external and the three] secret vehicles." Thus the commentaries [by Abhayākaragupta and Bhāvabhadra] accept the reading "external and secret [and three vehicles]." The twelfth section of the *Ornament of the Vajra Essence Tantra* says:

> Those in the pure family of Lotus light obtain unsurpassed enlightenment by keeping the external, inner, and secret pledges.

Who, then, pledges to keep the good Dharma? This is the pledge [of those in the Lotus family]. "Great enlightenment" is [414] discriminating wisdom realizing that all phenomena lack own-being; what "comes from" there is the "great Lotus" Amitābha; it is "pure" because of being free of settling on grasped and grasper, and so forth; "[those in] the family" means those having Amitābha as their nature. The *Clusters of Quintessential Instructions* explains:

> The vows of those in Amitābha's family are "pure" because of being, in essence, words free from immorality. So discriminating wisdom "comes from" these.

The way you keep these doctrines is, as explained earlier, to keep them by not rejecting them with the thought, "These are of no use to me."

Taking Amoghasiddhi's Vows

> Those in the great, excellent, Action family keep perfect possession of all the vows, and as much as able, offer worship. [Vś 769.6]

They "offer" what? "Worship." Indicating that, it says "possession of all the vows," which means worship that is the possession of all external and secret worship. Just that [worship] is "the vows," as the *Clusters of Quintessential Instructions* says:

> Here "vows" [mean] Amoghasiddhi family worship because [Amoghasiddhi is] the essence of transcendental knowledge [that causes] application [to practice].[53]

They keep them "perfectly." The *Clusters of Quintessential Instructions* explains:[54]

> External worship is five acts of service. Secret worship is when those holding their seed [syllable] and so forth in a meditational maṇḍala worship.

True reality worship is actualizing the state cleansed of the afflictions through embracing a partner and producing the four ecstasies that come about one after the other. The *Continuation of the Explanation of the Saṃvara Tantra* says of highest, true reality worship:

> When those habituated to the ground of no own-being meditate on a deity's heart, it is held to be the great worship, [415] the realization of all buddhas.

Hence it says that it is their [nondual] worship, [which they offer by] meditating on the [ultimate nature of] bodhicitta, their deity's essential nature—a state totally free of essential own-being.

These worship pledges are common to both [yoga and highest yoga] tantra and should be construed in a contextually appropriate manner.

How should they [keep] the pledge? They commit themselves "as much as they are able," or as much as it is in their power. The "and" is contingent on the earlier, [i.e., equate vows and worship]. Whose pledges are they? They are the pledges of "those in the great, supreme, Action family," of those in the form of Amoghasiddhi.

Summarizing the Commitment

> Having produced the highest, supreme bodhicitta, I will keep all vows for the sake of all living beings. I will free those not free, liberate those not liberated, give relief where there is no relief, and place living beings in nirvāṇa.

The first two lines ["having produced the highest, supreme bodhicitta"] sum up prayer bodhicitta and the bodhicitta after setting out. The next two lines ["I will keep all the vows for the sake of all living beings"] sum up the vows of the five [families]. "Free those not free" refers to those such as Brahmā and so forth who are bound by the ties of unawareness, that is, the two obscurations [afflictive obscurations and obscurations to knowledge]. "Liberate" from obscurations to knowledge "those" śrāvakas and pratyekabuddhas "not liberated" from them, "give relief" wherever "there is no relief," meaning the hells and so forth, "place" all "living beings in" nonabiding "nirvāṇa." This is the intention of both the *Clusters of Quintessential Instructions* and [Bhāvabhadra's] *Commentary on the Vajraḍāka*

Tantra. In the *Cluster of Quintessential Instructions* the latter verse ["I will free those not free...place living beings in nirvāṇa"] is talking about the bodhicitta after setting out. [416] Thus [my] explanation of the unclear passages, from Vairocana's vows on down, follows Bhāvabhadra's interpretation.

Ācārya Munendrabhadra says there are fourteen [vows]. In the Tathāgata family the Three Jewels are taken as one. In the Vajra family the vajra, bell-mudrā, and master are taken as three. In the Jewel family there are the four gifts. In the Lotus family there are four—external doctrine and the three vehicles. In the Action family [there are two]—being in possession of all the vows and offering worship. "Bell-mudrā," combining [the bell and mudrā] into one, contradicts the master Ānandagarbha's *Long Śrīparamādya Commentary,* which takes them to be separate, and so is wrong. It is also unlikely that his explanation of external [Dharma] in the Lotus family is correct. His mention of two in the Action family, however, does accord with the twelfth section of the *Ornament of the Vajra Essence Tantra,* which says:

> Many in Dundubhi's Action family possess the pledges and vows, serve and worship, and work for the welfare of living beings whereby they attain all his qualities.

There is also mention here of working for the welfare of living beings. Still, the above [explanation I have given] is the explanation in both [Bhāvabhadra's and Abhayākaragupta's] systems.

While it is true that all practitioners of each family must protect all the pledges, they should make a particular effort in regard to the pledges of their own particular family. Buddhaguhya in this *Introduction to the Meaning of the Tantras:*

> Those propitiating a deity, in whatever the family, should follow all those particular pledges indicated to do with the families as much as they are able, [417] with the qualification that they must make a special effort when it comes to the pledges to do with their own deity to be propitiated.

For example, if they are practitioners whose flower landed on Akṣobhya,[55] or on that family, then they should make a special effort to keep the three pledges and the master pledge.

Why are all the common pledges listed when listing the vows but not mentioned when the vows are taken? Some masters such as Lawapa [in his *Saṃvara Maṇḍala Ritual*] do, in fact, have [their disciples] take them after they have taken the five family vows. The ritual is not flawed, however, even if they do not do it separately when they are giving the vows. This is because if, after the master has given a synopsis of the general and individual pledges of the five families, the practitioners connected to the families strongly wish to receive ordination with the idea, "I will train in every one of the pledges to be trained in," this is sufficient for the ordination to come into being.

So then, summarizing the texts on taking [tantric] vows, we have the following. Having taken refuge in the Three Jewels and your teachers, you produce the great mudrā, which is yourself in the form of the deity. Recollecting—that is, taking up the vajra and bell's true reality—you offer worship to yourself, and, through mastering [the teachings of] the three vehicles, refrain from all immorality, bring together all wholesome dharmas, and work for the welfare of living beings through the four gifts.

In his *Maṇḍala Ritual* Nāgabodhi says, "The disciple and the guru, [418] having first said three times..." Thus both disciple and master should each recite the ritual ordination passage three times. Similarly, Rahulaśrīmitra's *[Clarification of Union] Maṇḍala Ritual* and the *Vajrāvalī of Maṇḍala Rituals* also say they have to do it three times—so it must be said three times. It is imperative to do all three times especially for first-time ordination or to restore broken [vows]. This is because, it seems to me, as elsewhere [such as in the Vinaya rituals], if there is not the completion [of the three recitations], the ritual act is not completed and [the ordination] does not come into being.

Why does it say to take the vows again and again even if you have already taken them and have not given them up? This is to make your intention to protect the vows strong. The *Introduction to the Meaning of the Tantras* says:

> Although Definitions [Vehicle] Mahāyāna vows revealed in the shared ritual have already been impressed upon your mind, to make your mind strong again, produce them in the presence of the Lord.

[Here is an explanation of] when the vows are taken. The two *Twenty Verse Rituals,*[56] the *Clarification of Union Maṇḍala Ritual,* and the *Vajrāvalī of Maṇḍala Rituals* have the ordination toward the end of the preparatory day. The masters Ānandagarbha and so forth follow the *Vajra Tip Tantra* and say it is on the day of consecration proper. Dīpaṃkarabhadra [in his *Guhyasamāja Maṇḍala Ritual*] says:

> Inquire about the quality of the dream and using skillful means destroy the unwholesome. Then have the well-guarded disciple who has become a receptacle keep the vows.

He thus has the ordination after the inquiry about the disciple's dreams and before the consecration proper gets underway, and many follow him in this. It is clear that regardless of which of these is followed for taking [the ordination, it] comes into being. The ordination comes into being at the end of saying the ordination ritual passage three times [419]. It is not contingent on the completion of the consecration.

These [perspectives] are from the point of view of [vows] taken in connection with a maṇḍala ritual. Not included are others—for example, those taken when cultivating clear realization. Since those are spoken of a little bit differently in the *Kālacakra Tantra,* I will discuss them later.

This completes the explanation of taking the vows.

3. Vows and Consecrations

THIS SECTION has three parts: not consecrating those not taking vows; having dealt with objections to that, taking the vows through consecration; and which vows are taken in action and performance tantra consecrations.

Not Consecrating Those Not Taking Vows

[Ānandagarbha's] *Maṇḍala Ritual Called Sarvavajrodaya* says:

> Do not say "Today, I...you..." [i.e., the words of the actual consecration] to those who are not keeping the vows. Do not give permission or consecration to them as a master. Just let them gain entry.

This says that you just let those who are not keeping the ordination enter [into consecration] up until the casting of the flower and identification of their deity, without giving [the actual] consecration. And while you let them enter, you refrain from the solemn promises section [of the ritual] as well.[57] Similarly, you should also set aside the request for ordination, and so on. It also says it is unnecessary to examine whether or not they are receptacles when you are just letting them enter. The *Vajraśekara Tantra* [850.5–851.2] says:

> It is right to let each and every sort of living being enter into this great, royal, secret maṇḍala of all tathāgatas. Do not investigate whether they are receptacles or not because you must keep those who are attracted to gaining entry. [420] And why? Because just by seeing [a maṇḍala] all living beings become irreversible [from enlightenment]. Even though many are indeed without faith, without the accumulation of a root of virtue, with an unripened

> mindstream, and lacking belief, still, just by seeing [a maṇḍala], this is so.

Thus of the two—letting them enter the maṇḍala and bestowing consecration on them after entry—it says that you are not prohibited from letting those who are not receptacles enter, but are prohibited from bestowing consecration on them. As it says in the *Vajra Tip Tantra,* "Give entry to those who are not receptacles," and, "Just give entry, do not do everything." Hence when [the *Vajra Tip Tantra* and *Maṇḍala Ritual Called Sarvavajrodaya*'s] root tantra, *Compendium of Principles,* says, "When giving entry to this great maṇḍala do not examine whether or not they are receptacles," it intends what its explanatory tantra, the *Vajra Tip Tantra,* says it means. This is what the scholar Ānandagarbha has said [in his *Illumination of the "Compendium of Principles"*].

Is just letting them enter the maṇḍala without giving consecration correct in other tantra sets [besides yoga tantra] as well? [In response] in *Great Vairocana's Enlightenment Discourse* [a performance tantra], it says:

> Lord of Secrets! It is only with respect to those Vajrasattvas who have already become habituated to the Mahāyāna tantric lifestyle through infinite doors of practice that this specific number has been given. However, a master with great compassion commits to liberating [421] absolutely every living creature, and retains infinite living beings because [it produces] the bodhicitta that is a cause.

The *Commentary* on this [by Buddhaguhya] says:

> The above specification of number is in regard to disciples who are to be ripened into adepts or masters. [The master] also produces great compassion for all beings other than those, even though, when they are let into the maṇḍala, they will not become masters or adepts. So [the master] retains infinite, innumerable [living beings] because, when they are let in and produce bodhicitta, it is the seed cause of enlightenment.

He explains that the mention of a specific number of supreme disciples like that is "because they are rare and few and far between." Buddhaguhya thus holds that this practice [of just letting them enter the maṇḍala] is acceptable in both action and performance tantras as well, because he says:

> Even though *Great Vairocana's Enlightenment Discourse* is first a skill in means performance tantra, it is also demonstrably like an action tantra or a yoga tantra.

The *Illumination of* (the first part of) *the "Compendium of Principles"* says:

> Why is it not the case here as it is in action tantra? What reasons are there? [Intending] this, the *[Compendium of Principles]* tantra here says "Why...".

And the *Commentary on the Compendium of Principles, Ornament of Kosala* says, "Here do not investigate whether the person is a receptacle or not, as you do in other tantras where there is an examination of whether they are or are not receptacles."

It is incorrect to interpret these statements to mean that there is no need here [in yoga tantra] to carry out the examination of disciples necessary when letting them into action and performance tantra maṇḍalas, because the reasons given [in yoga tantra for dispensing with the examination—namely] that there is a great purpose if the three irreligious persons and the religious person are let in—are applicable in action and performance tantra as well. [422] So, in action and performance tantra those who do not like pledges and who are incapable of the above conduct are unsuitable for consecration or unsuitable as receptacles for the path, while the opposite [is true of] those who are receptacles. Just as there is a need [in all three tantra sets for that], similarly there is no need [to investigate whether disciples are or are not receptacles] when they are [just] entering a maṇḍala. You have to construe it thus, so it is apparent that the master Ānandagarbha, other [yoga tantra writers], and Buddhaguhya are the same [in what they say about the question of mere entrance].

[Śāntipa] cites the *Compendium of Principles* in his *Jewel Lamp Commentary* on the *Black Yamāri Tantra,* explaining that you just let those who stop [the immorality of] killing enter [the maṇḍala]; you place those who do not stop in equilibrium, or else you let them enter with force. This explains that this practice [of just letting them enter] is suitable in highest yoga tantra as well [because the *Black Yamāri Tantra* is a highest yoga tantra].

Having Dealt with Objections to That, Taking the Vows Through Consecration

Question: The *Maṇḍala Ritual Called Sarvavajrodaya* and the *Illumination of* (the first part of) *the "Compendium of Principles"* prohibit consecrating those who are not taking vows. The same commentary [the *Illumination*] says that consecration can be given to those not taking vows:

> The flower garland consecration, mudrā consecration, vajra consecration, owner[58] consecration, and name consecration that are spoken of are all for the purpose of producing the seed of irreversibility. So they are general consecrations for those who have taken and those who have not taken mantra vows.

Is it not the case that these two are contradictory? [In response we say] there is no contradiction. The "just" in [the *Maṇḍala Ritual Called Sarvavajrodaya*'s] "Just let them gain entry" cuts out consecration relative to those without Dharma who do not take mantra vows, as in the *Vajra Tip Tantra* cited earlier [419–20]. The statement in the *Illumination of* (the first part of) *the "Compendium of Principles"* is relative to the disciple consecrations of a disciple who, though not taking mantra vows, is still a suitable receptacle for the disciple consecrations. So without mantra vows, it is definite that the vajra master consecration cannot be given [423], but the disciple consecrations can either be given or not given.

Which disciple is suitable for just disciple consecrations? A certain scholar says [that these are] "those who want to attain accomplishments having taken just the disciple consecration."[59] This is not right. Rather, you should assert what Śāntipa says in his *Commentary on [Dīpaṃkarabhadra's] Guhyasamāja Maṇḍala Ritual:*

> To whom [do masters] give just the knowledge consecration? They [give it] to those who do not strive for consecration as master or to those who, while striving, are yet made to take the general minor ordination but not the master ordination.

Thus he says that those with just disciple consecration are those who, whether or not they strive for consecration as a master, take only the shared ordination and do not take the master ordination. Further, about these two ordinations, the same *Commentary* says:

> The vows that are given to those who are not acting as masters are the general ones marked by just the aforementioned refuge and production of bodhicitta. The vows that are given to those who are acting as masters are the master ordination systematized as the five family [pledges].

Thus he says that those striving for master consecration and those striving for just disciple consecration both have to take refuge-based bodhicitta vows. These are therefore shared or general vows. The five family vows taken with the passage that begins, "Just as the lords of the three times..." [Vś 769.2–3] are not, however, given when it is just a disciple consecration, [424] but are given in master consecrations. This position is also set forth in the *Vajrāvalī of Maṇḍala Rituals* and in [Ratnarakṣita's] *Padminī Commentary on the Saṃvarodaya Tantra,* which seems to be based on these two [texts]. It is excellent.

So, as the *Compendium of Principles* and its *Illumination* say, those just let into the maṇḍala take neither shared nor uncommon vows. They are those who do the five criminal acts that incur immediate retribution who have a powerful greed for things of a political nature, for food and drink, and for the five sense experiences, who do not delight in keeping the solemnly promised pledges, who are incapable of the eighteen preliminaries, who are scared of the training rules for householders, and who have an interest in gaining entrance into the maṇḍala of ordinary deities such as Mahādeva. In the *Ornament of Kosala* it says that [these practitioners] are not precluded from taking refuge and producing bodhicitta, because by doing so and entering the maṇḍala they will obtain all good qualities. The bodhicitta must be just prayer bodhicitta, however, because were it the bodhicitta after setting out that is taken by means of a ritual, they would have taken the shared vows. Therefore you should not do what pertains to the shared vows with them either [i.e., in the ritual have them make the request and so forth]. Understand just what an excellent way this is to leave a positive impression on those who are not capable of keeping vows, but are interested in mantra.

Here they are saying that taking the two [types of] vows [shared and uncommon] or not taking them is governed by the consideration that vows, once taken, are meant to be kept. The nonsensical ritual taking of vows where they are not kept [425] is not an issue. You give consecrations commensurate with the capacity to keep vows. It is therefore saying that you should not bestow the master consecration on those who do not keep the five family vows or mantra vows they have taken, even if they ask for it. So obviously you do not bestow anything higher than that.

According to Śāntipa (and Abhayākara and Ratnarakṣita and many others also), the shared vows are given with the lines:

> I go for refuge to the Three Jewels. I make a confession of each and every wrong. I rejoice in the virtues of the world. I take the Buddha's enlightenment to heart.

The first three sentences teach the preliminary practices and the fourth teaches bodhicitta, as in[60] "With the arising of all the fine qualities of the maṇḍala ritual, the production of the thought of Buddha's enlightenment..."

And since just prayer bodhicitta is not enough for ordination, this must be referring to the production of bodhicitta after setting out, so the lama must spell out the meaning of the lines clearly.

As for the ordination ritual, there are many versions, such as the one in the *Vajra Tent Tantra* and so forth, so the exact wording of the ritual is not definite. When it is taken by means of a few lines such as the above, [four lines beginning, "I go for refuge to the Three Jewels,"] the intended recipient is an extremely gifted person who comprehends the fact that an ordination is being taken with just that. Abhayākara states, "It says, 'I go for refuge to the Buddha, Dharma, and Supreme Community from now until enlightenment.'"

The finest of the gifted persons are caused to produce bodhicitta, the essence of which is an ordination, with just this summary version thinking, "Based on going for refuge to the Form Body, the Dharma Body, and the Community of irreversible bodhisattvas, I will myself become a perfect buddha, and, [426] having brought out the entire world from suffering, I will secure them in the state of a perfect buddha."

The *Vajra Tip Tantra:*

> When they keep the householder ordination forsaking murder, theft, fornication, lying, and getting drunk they will become kings of the sciences. Were they to have gone forth to homelessness, perfectly keeping the three ordinations (the prātimokṣa, bodhisattva, and knowledge-holder vows) they would be supreme.

This says that those gone forth to homelessness—the basis for tantric practice—should take the three ordinations. It is not, however, saying that the householder tantric practitioner does not have the three ordinations. [They do,] because [the *Vajra Tip Tantra*] says they have to keep to the householder training [one of the prātimokṣa ordinations], and before taking tantric vows they have to take bodhisattva vows. Still [the wording of the *Vajra Tip Tantra*] reflects the fact that of the prātimokṣa [ordinations], the ordinations of those gone forth to homelessness are the main ones, and [the householders] do not have those. And the *Vajra Tip Tantra* says, "Having given [them] the three ordinations, then reveal the maṇḍala."

Thus those practicing the paths of the two higher tantra sets have to do so on the basis of their prātimokṣa vows, and where they are suitable vessels, within keeping the three ordinations. And it is particularly important that they take the bodhisattva ordination. The maṇḍala rituals reiterate this, but still I have given this explanation because there are few presentations formulated in such a way that they remove all doubt about it.

The two verses ["When they keep the householder ordination...they would be supreme"] cited earlier are absent from some [editions of the] *Vajra Tip Tantra*. Still, they are authentic because they are in some [editions], and [427] many writers such as Buddhaguhya cite them as an extract from that tantra. The master Ānandagarbha teaches that all of the shared vows are taken on the preparatory day through producing the thought of enlightenment and making a commitment to train in bodhisattva conduct.

Which Vows Are Taken in Action and Performance Tantra Consecrations

The *Vajrāvalī of Maṇḍala Rituals* says:

> These six—garland, water, and so forth—consecrations cause the antidote to ignorance to become effective, so they are called

> the knowledge consecration. These consecrations empower a disciple to listen to, explain, and practice the mantras in action and performance tantra.

[Ratnarakṣita's] *Padminī Commentary on the Saṃvarodaya Tantra* explains in a similar fashion. According to Abhayākara, therefore, for consecration in the *Bhūtadamaka* and other maṇḍalas that he sets forth in his *Vajrāvalī of Maṇḍala Rituals* (excluding the consecrations into maṇḍalas of the two highest tantra sets [taught there]), it is sufficient if, having set aside the taking of vows to be kept in the five family ordination, you bestow consecration after they have taken just the shared vows. This is because the mere disciple consecration empowers them to listen to, explain, and practice action and performance tantras, and because you do not give vajra master ordination unless you have bestowed the master consecration. Master Lawapa's *Maṇḍala Ritual* says:

> Thus if they simply want the five knowledge consecrations, you give them, without having them take the aforementioned master ordination. Immediately after that you give the four: permission, particular rules, prophecy, and reliefs.

Thus he says that if you bestow nothing beyond just the disciple consecrations [428], you do not make them take the five family ordination.

So, the masters Ānandagarbha, Lawapa, Śāntipa, Abhayākara, and Ratnarakṣita all assert that if you bestow nothing beyond just the disciple consecration, you do not make them take the five family vows. It is therefore wrong to take the five family ordination in action and performance tantra. And since in the absence of that, the uncommon mantra ordination is not present, in action and performance tantra there are two ordinations: the bodhisattva ordination and, in some cases, a prātimokṣa ordination.

Vāgīśvarakīrti [in his *Reality Shining Like a Jewel*], Rahulaśrīmitra [in his *Clarification of Union*], and Nandivajra [in his *Explanation of the Empowerment*] say that the five water consecrations and so forth and the sixth master consecration are not excluded in action and performance tantras. The master consecration they are referring to is the way of giving the four: the permission, particular vajra rules, prophecy, and reliefs that come at the end of the five knowledge consecrations [and are called the boundary base].[61] The master Buddhaguhya says the statement in the

Great Vairocana's Enlightenment Discourse, "Give the wheel and conch and give them permission to explain the doctrine," is referring to a master consecration. The *All Secrets Tantra* says:

> Then meditate thus: Now, become a maṇḍala master, I will also hold secret mantra tantras. Honored by all the buddhas, bodhisattvas, and gods, out of pity for living beings, I must, in accord with the ritual, rouse myself, draw the maṇḍala, and connect practitioners with the tantra as well.

This says that, having been given permission to explain the drawing of a maṇḍala, you become a maṇḍala master. And it says [elsewhere] that if you have been consecrated in the Tathāgata family maṇḍala you become [429] a vajra master for all three families. [These, from Vāgīśvarakīrti's text to the *All Secrets Tantra*], intend the consecration that lets you act specifically as an action and performance tantra master [and not as a full vajra master with the five family ordination].

Abhayākara and Ratnarakṣita, speaking about action and performance tantras in general, say that when you bestow nothing beyond the mere disciple consecration, you also make the boundary base[62] as before and with just that consecration consecrate [the disciple] to listen to, explain, and practice the mantras of action and performance tantras. They do not distinguish between individual action and performance tantra consecrations. The twelfth section of the *Ornamental Spot of Wisdom Tantra* does say there are a different number of consecrations in action and performance tantras:

> The sequence of the three tantras teaches the six consecration division. The water and ornament consecrations are well-known in action tantra. The vajra, bell, and name are made clear in performance tantra. Yoga tantra elucidates the irreversible consecration. That is the six-particular consecration. That is the master consecration.

The master consecration that they have said is absent is the vajra master consecration in which the five family vows are taken, not the consecration [in action and performance tantra] that simply lets you function as a vajra master.

A certain learned person gives the following explanation of "That is the six-particular":

> It is not saying that there are the earlier five and then the master consecration as the sixth. The irreversible consecration, secret consecration, permission, prophecy, reliefs, and praise are the master consecration itself made into six. The earlier five [beginning with water] and these make eleven, plus there are the last three consecrations for a total of fourteen. Thus that *[Ornamental Spot of Wisdom Tantra]* says, "There are two [430] seven-particulars..." Thus it says that from the water up until the fourth there are a total of fourteen consecrations.

Therefore, when it comes to consecration, in the two upper tantra sets it is done with double consecration as vajra master and vajra disciple. In the lower [sets], however, except for the water consecration and so forth, which are widely known as the "upper-set-vajra-disciple consecration," along with the boundary base [i.e., the permission and so forth], there is no separate vajra master consecration. The [mere] vajra master consecration is included in just that [vajra disciple consecration]. The names are the same, but since the water consecrations and so on differ in content even in the upper [sets], it goes without saying that there are different meanings for them in the lower [sets] as well.

Therefore, the following statements contradict the texts of the great. [1] Padmāṅkuśa states in his *Maṇḍala Ritual of the Protectress with the White Parasol,* after [saying that the master] should make them take the five family ordination, that his position is that you bestow four water, headdress, vajra, and bell consecrations not unlike the ones in highest [yoga tantras]. Others take a different position [and say] that there are name and irreversibility consecrations, too. [2] Vajrasaṃnāha and others make statements about taking a five-family ordination.

Most other learned authors of action and performance tantra evocations and rituals mention taking the bodhicitta [ordination] without taking the five family ordination. Accept that as correct.

Hence in the case of action or performance tantra consecrations, although there are many shared pledges, still, when there is an infraction, the Mahāyāna vows that define the parameters of root downfalls are the bodhisattva vows and bodhisattva vows alone. You should realize that a root downfall occurs in relation to those vows and protect them accordingly. Were this not the case, and were you to assert that you take the vows by taking [431] the five family ordination, the consecrations given would have to be the consecrations from the master consecration on up, and the root downfalls would have to be the fourteen root downfalls [of the higher tantras], because when there is the proclamation of those vows, it lists those fourteen downfalls.

As for the *Compendium of All the Pledges* statement:

> The enumeration of them is as follows: four shared root downfalls, twelve Perfection root downfalls, thirty action tantra root downfalls, fourteen performance tantra root downfalls, fourteen yoga tantra root downfalls, fourteen root downfalls, plus five and four for a total of seventy.

You cannot feel certain about this. Not only is the addition faulty (the total should be ninety-seven, not seventy), but it also says [elsewhere] in regard to how to restore [broken pledges] that if you harm your master's pledge you [simply] enter into a maṇḍala, and [even] if you harm your vajra relative pledge you do not need a [new] consecration. It says other things as well that I shall refute below. Even though we find in certain editions the reading, "thirteen action tantra root downfalls," still it does not add up.

After the death of Jowo Chenpo [Atiśa], Nagpo Damtsigdorje came to Tibet. He and the translator Nagtso did many translations as a team. Since in this [*Compendium of All the Pledges* colophon] it says "...from the mouth of my teacher, the blessed Damtsigdorje...," it would mainly appear to be that teacher's communications.[63] There is a mixture of something from here with something from there. One way or the other, Jowo Chenpo is not the author [of the *Compendium of All the Pledges*].

A certain scholar, taking the number of root downfalls that this *[Compendium of All the Pledges]* teaches to be authoritative, says that the fourteen performance tantra root downfalls are the four that *Great Vairocana's Enlightenment Discourse* says are root downfalls, and the ten unwholesome actions [432] that are explained as harming the vows and cutting them from the root. He is incorrect, because *Great Vairocana's Enlightenment Discourse* says:

> Lord! Please explain to us about bodhisattvas who harm and cut the root of the ten wholesome action paths ordination, how even bodhisattvas who are supreme rulers over temporal affairs and experience human and divine pleasures in the company of householders, sons and daughters, and near and distant relations do not incur downfalls.

Thus it asks [1] what harms and cuts the root of the ten wholesome action paths ordination and [2] how lay bodhisattvas involved in politics still do not incur a root downfall. It does not mention "ten unwholesome actions." Also [Buddhaguhya's] *Commentary* on this says:

> There, "[Please explain to us about bodhisattvas] who harm... the ten wholesome action paths ordination." Please explain to us about bodhisattvas who have received the five-discipline [householder] ordination: to what extent do they not have the ten wholesome action paths ordination?

In response *Great Vairocana's Enlightenment Discourse* says:

> Guhyaka Adhipati, listen to this and take it well to heart. This is the explanation of those expert in the Bodhisattva Vinaya downfalls. Guhyaka Adhipati, there are two sorts of bodhisattvas. Who are these two? They are the householder bodhisattvas and the bodhisattvas gone forth to homelessness. Among them, householder bodhisattvas stay home, keep the five bases of training [433], and rule over temporal affairs in a variety of ways. Guhyaka Adhipati, those bodhisattvas, governed by time and place and wishing for omniscience, demonstrate all sorts of songs, music, dazzling sights, and so forth, properly informed by means. With these ways and means they attract living beings through the four ways of attracting disciples. This is because of their wish for unsurpassed, perfect enlightenment. They forsake murder, robbery, sexual deviancy caused by obsessive attraction, lying, and wrong view. Those householder bodhisattvas keep the five bases of training, training in the training that has been taught. They should faithfully train as did the tathāgatas of long ago.

This responds to the later question.

> Stationed in the unconditioned morality aggregate praised by the unsurpassed Tathāgata, and, in their conditioned morality, behaving in a fashion informed by method and wisdom, they would not degenerate into the four root downfalls even for the sake of their life. What are the four? They are forsaking the holy Dharma, giving up bodhicitta, being miserly, and harming living beings. And why? Because those are bereft of means and wisdom, are in their nature afflicted, and are not restorable.

This responds to the first question. Here [434] it talks not about the bases of training of those gone forth to homelessness, but about the training of the householders, because the root downfalls that sever bodhisattva morality are the same for both. This is because you can understand them from the explanation about householders, and because, while there is no need here to teach the prātimokṣa root downfalls [of monks and nuns], it is necessary to provide an answer to the question further on that makes particular reference to householders.

The *Bodhisattva Levels* explains the last two of the [four] root downfalls,[64] the *Ākāśagarbha Sūtra* says the first is a root downfall, and the *Skillful Means Sūtra* says the second is. Therefore they are root downfalls relative to bodhisattva vows. I have dealt with these at length in my *[Basic Path to Awakening]* explanation of the morality chapter [of the *Bodhisattva Levels*]. Read about them there.

[Guhyaka Adhipati] asks two things in "[Please explain to us about bodhisattvas] who [1] harm and [2] cut the root of the vows of the ten wholesome [action paths]." [Buddhaguhya's] *Commentary* says the first is relative to bodhisattvas who receive the five-discipline [householder ordination] from others, and the second relative to bodhisattvas who do not receive the five-discipline [householder ordination] from others, but by themselves make a commitment to protect bodhicitta. In the former case, the four root downfalls harm the ten wholesome actions ordination [i.e., bodhisattva ordination], but they retain their [householder] prātimokṣa ordinations, while in the latter case neither ordinations remain and there is severance from the root. This is what is intended, so the reading "[harm] and do not cut the root"[65] found in some editions is corrupt.

[Buddhaguhya's] *Commentary* gives a general explanation [of the four root downfalls relative to the bodhisattva, or ten wholesome action paths, ordination]. [1] "Forsaking the holy Dharma" is wrong view [in the sense of] removing the importance Dharma has in your life,[66] denigrating it and those who explain it, and desisting, each day, from listening to, thinking about, meditating on, asking about, reading, or worshipping the Dharma. [2] "Giving up bodhicitta" is giving up meditation on the emptiness of prayer bodhicitta and the bodhicitta after setting out. [3] "Being miserly" is not giving when you have Dharma and wealth and it is appropriate [435] to give it to others. "Harming living beings" is causing immediate or lasting harm to living beings physically, verbally, or mentally. You can understand why they become root downfalls [by reading] elsewhere [in my *Basic Path to Awakening*].

"They are not restorable" does not mean you cannot take the ordination again if you have given it up. What it does mean is that when there are the earlier three and harming living beings out of a feeling of hatred, based on those conditions you would be in an essentially afflicted state where more leeway is given [and you would not be pushed to retake the ordination because you could never keep it].

Great Vairocana's Enlightenment Discourse presents the way to take the ten wholesome actions ordination. There is the request, "Which vows, unobscured during the three times, are the vows that delight the buddhas and bodhisattvas?" In response it says, "These are where you give your self to the Victor and the bodhisattvas. When you have given that, you have given your body, speech, and mind and have [to keep] the vows of body, speech, and mind as a bodhisattva."

[Buddhaguhya's] *Commentary* explains that this means that when you have given yourself to the buddhas and bodhisattvas you are no longer in charge—they are. And since in their system they do not engage in immorality, the ordination is thus taken. [He says] the vows that are unobscured during the three times are the vows to desist from the ten unwholesome actions. Since in other texts they are referred to as "ordination morality," this indicates taking the three moralities: [the training in morality,] the morality that brings together wholesome dharmas, [and the morality of working for the welfare of living beings].

In the *Three Pledges Array Tantra* there is a lucid ritual for taking the ordination by giving yourself away. It is spoken in the context of taking the ordination when entering into the maṇḍala.

There, to take the pledges and vows say the following three times:

> All buddhas and bodhisattvas please listen to me. I, named so-and-so [436], give myself to all buddhas and bodhisattvas. At all times please take hold of me well. Buddhas and bodhisattvas, please work through me. Compassionate ones, saviors of all living beings, please save me. In order that all the work may be accomplished, please let me take this pledge.

Again Ānandagarbha in his *Commentary on the Net of Illusion Tantra* says:

> "I take to heart the Buddha's enlightenment" teaches bodhicitta. Understand that since you have already given yourself away it does not mention it separately. It is saying that somebody who has produced bodhicitta has completely given everything.

And the *All Secrets Tantra,* after saying, "That night set out to take such vows to the extent that you are able," says:

> Take refuge in the Three Foremost. Then produce the unsurpassed[67] bodhicitta that has not been produced, and remember those already produced.

Śāntipa in his *Commentary on [Dīpaṃkarabhadra's] Guhyasamāja Maṇḍala Ritual* sets forth this latter verse [from the *All Secrets Tantra*] and says that it is the ordination ritual for taking the shared vows. In the *Mañjuśrī Root Tantra* it also says:

> Mantra conduct becomes perfect when you have three dharmas. What are these three? [437] They are not totally forsaking all living beings, protecting the vows of bodhisattva morality, and not totally forsaking your mantra.

Thus [in all of these tantras and commentaries] it is clear that in action and performance tantra rituals for taking the supreme vehicle ordination there is just taking the ordination [connected with the ritual production of bodhicitta] after setting out, not the five family ordination. So you should understand without any reservation that the vows taken [in action and performance tantras] are the bodhisattva vows. Hence you cannot feel confidence in the explanation in the summarizing *Ratnāvalī Commentary* said to have been composed by Śāntipa[68] that the five family ordination is taken as an adjunct to the ritual for taking the master ordination after having taken disciple ordination in the disciple consecrations. It stands contradicted by the texts of the great ones.

In present times, although there do not seem to be many performance tantra consecrations, many action tantra consecrations are given. On those occasions, few pay attention to how the vows are taken and what root downfalls are to be protected against. I have noticed that [those occasions] are not informed by [an awareness of] whether vows are, or are not, to be taken, and if they are taken, of the limit beyond which transgression does, or does not, occur. So I have given this explanation with the thought that it is just for that occasional person with a serious interest in the vows of the Superior Vehicle who might come along.

In summary: Just let people who keep no ordination into the maṇḍala and bestow absolutely none of the consecrations from the water on up. Even if they have taken, and are keeping, the bodhisattva vows, but will not keep the five family ordination after taking it, bestow the water consecration and so forth, but do not bestow any of the the consecrations from vajra master on up. As the fifteenth chapter of the *Vajra Tent Tantra,* as cited in the *Vajrāvalī of Maṇḍala Rituals* says, there is a specific order to this:

> First is the water consecration, second [438] the headdress consecration, third, the consecration by the vajra. Fourth is your master, fifth the name consecration, and sixth the state of a complete buddha. Seventh is the vase consecration, eighth the secret consecration, and ninth the wisdom consecration—through true reality vajra practice the rule that all is the vajra[69] is given. [Then] the prophecy of oneself as the [enlightened] teacher. These are the sequence in the consecration rituals.

This completes my presentation of the issue of which consecrations are to be bestowed when vows are or are not kept.

4. Root Downfalls

SECOND, determining the downfalls that break the vows to which you have committed yourself, is in three parts: identifying the basis [i.e., person] in whose mindstream downfalls occur, the divisions of promise-breaking downfalls in that person, and the explanation of each of the divisions.

Identifying the Basis

First, [about the person], two features are required: the person must have taken an uncommon, secret mantra ordination and not given it up, and the person must be sane. The first of these is necessary because, although those without ordination can do wrong that is immorality in and of itself, they cannot be guilty of promise-breaking downfalls. [The second is necessary because] if they are mad and out of their wits they cannot be guilty of a downfall. This is similar to the explanations given in the bodhisattva vow section of the *Bodhisattva Levels*.[70]

The Divisions of Downfalls

Second [about the divisions], the *Vajrāvalī of Maṇḍala Rituals* says,[71] "Downfalls of those who have Vajrasattva ordination are of two sorts: root downfalls and gross downfalls."[72]

This division into two "sorts" of categories is good because the *Kālacakra Tantra* and its [439] *Stainless Light Commentary*, the *Saṃvarodaya Tantra*, and *Vajra Tip Tantra* use these two designations and none other.

Explanation of the Subdivisions

This has two parts: explanation of the downfalls in highest yoga tantras other than the *Kālacakra Tantra,* and [the explanation] in that tantra. The first has two parts: explanation of the root and the gross downfalls. The first of these again has two parts: the meaning of the title [of the text used as a basis for the explanation] and the meaning of the text.

The Explanation of the Downfalls in Highest Yoga Tantras Other than the Kālacakra Tantra

The Root Downfalls

The Meaning of the Title

First, the title is *Vajra Vehicle Root Downfalls.* "Vajrayāna." As Śāntipa says in his *Handful of Flowers Commentary* on the statement in the fifteenth part of the *Guhyasamāja Tantra* that "the Vajrayāna is unsurpassed":

> "Vajrayāna." The entire Mahāyāna is collected within the six perfections. They in turn are collected within skillful means and wisdom, and these are collected within the single taste that is bodhicitta. That is the Vajrasattva meditative stabilization and just that is the vajra. It is a *vajra* and it is a *yāna;* hence a *Vajrayāna,*[73] a Mantrayāna.

Thus Vajrasattva[74] practice that is the coming together of skillful means and wisdom indivisibly is the vajra, and it is the vehicle as well. There are two of them—the causal vehicle by means of which you go [i.e., get there], and the resultant vehicle in which you go [when you are there]. The tantric ordination [constitutes the vehicle] by means of which you go. The promise-breaking karmic hindrance[75] of those who have that [ordination] is a downfall[76] because it leads them down and because it hinders the arising of good qualities. It is modified by the epithet "root" because it is a downfall that severs [i.e., uproots] the ordination when incurred, that goes as deep as can be gone. Do not take "root" in the sense of the root of siddhis when protected and the root of misery when not protected,[77] because in [the Tibetan translations of] both *Great Vairocana's Enlightenment Discourse* and the *Ākāśagarbha Sūtra,* [440] we find the translation "root of the downfall,"[78] and so you have to take "root" as something to get rid of. It could not be the root of a downfall were it something to protect in the sense of the root of siddhis. And [Mañjuśrīkīrti in his] *Commentary on the Root Downfalls* is not right when he says:

> Alternatively, it is a downfall because when the root of skillful means and wisdom has shriveled, you see unwanted results.

If you take the root of skillful means and wisdom and the root of a root downfall to be the same it leads to nonsense.

The Meaning of the Text

The meaning of the text has three parts: introductory activities, the composition of the explanation itself, and the conclusion.

Introduction

The first again has two parts: expression of worship and commitment to the undertaking.

First, the expression of worship:

> Having bowed down with complete respect to the lotus feet of my guru... [Mā 1ab]

"Having bowed down..." To what? Having bowed down to the feet, construed as a lotus, of the author's guru. Since it is the lowest part of his body, it indicates extreme respect. How? He bows with extreme respect motivated by deep faith and carried out through every door [i.e., bowing with the body, saying "I bow down," and thinking deeply reverent thoughts]. The reason he does so is because whenever holy beings set out to do something big, at the outset they bow down to, and worship, special objects [of worship, such as the Three Jewels]. So this is to conform to their behavior and to remove any hindrances that might occur. Many saintly gurus of previous times have said that this indicates that you should respectfully worship your special objects of refuge not only at the outset of writing something, but at the outset of any practice of spiritual activity.

Second, the commitment to the undertaking.

> ...I shall explain the fourteen root downfalls spoken [441] of in the tantras. [Mā 1cd]

"I shall explain..." What? ...the fourteen root downfalls. To those who say, You have just made it up yourself, so what you say cannot be trusted, [he responds] There is not that fault because I shall explain what is "spoken of in the tantras." A tantra[79] is a continuum[80] that persists, of which there are two: [tantric] texts that set forth [meanings], and [tantric] meanings that are set forth [in those texts]. Here it is the [tantric] texts that set forth [meanings].

The eighteenth part of the *Red Yamāri Tantra,* the seventeenth part of the *Black Yamāri Tantra,* and the twelfth section of the *Ornament of the Vajra Essence Tantra* speak about all fourteen [downfalls], while the fifteenth part of the *Vajra Tent Tantra* speaks about ten. There are many tantras that speak about other specific [downfalls] and so forth. I shall explain all those that the *Kālacakra Tantra* has spoken about [later].

Some earlier saints have said the following about the purpose of making such a commitment to write [a text]: Since saintly persons do not lightly commit themselves to just anything, and, once they have [committed themselves], do not give up until they completely finish what they have set out to do, we should therefore understand this to exemplify the commitment we have to bring to our ordination and so forth.

The Composition of the Explanation Itself

This has two parts: what to do so that you are not degraded by a downfall, and how to repair [a vow] if it is broken. The first has three parts: identifying the downfalls, producing the wish to protect yourself from being degraded by a downfall, and how to guard against that. Again the first has two parts: the explanation of each downfall and a summary. There are fourteen root downfalls. The explanation of the first of these downfalls has two parts: [442] a real [i.e., total] root downfall and a downfall in which the branches are not complete.

What to Do So You Are Not Degraded

Identifying the Downfalls

First Root Downfall

> Since the vajra holder said that siddhis flow from the masters,
> the first root downfall is said to be disparaging them. [Mā 2]

There are three parts to this: the object [relative to which the downfall is incurred, the action that causes the downfall, and the reason that disparaging the master in that fashion causes a downfall].

The Object [Relative to Which the Downfall Is Incurred]

They are your "masters," whomever they may be. Although the *Root Downfall Commentary Amṛtacandra*[81] and Lakṣmīṅkara's *Root Downfalls Commentary* say they have to have consecrated you, [Śāntipa's] *Jewel Lamp Commentary* on the *Black Yamāri Tantra* says:

> Are masters only those who have bestowed consecration? [Response:] Those who have bestowed a consecration, taught you a tantra, and those from whom you have received instructions about the activity [associated with the practice of that tantra] are masters. All three of these—free from envy and wanting to help—are masters.[82] Thus the verse: "Whoever reads, explains and gives instructions in the holy scriptures, bestows consecration and does the activity is a 'master.'"

And:

> Anyone who hears a single verse from someone and does not treat them as a guru takes birth as a dog a hundred times and then is reborn as a scorpion.

The master Kāmadhenu[83] [in his *Commentary on the Cleansing All States of Woe Tantra*] also mentions this threefold division of masters, and is correct when he says that foremost among them are those who bestow consecration. Thus there are three masters. In the *Ornament of Kosala,*

[Śākyamitra] cites both [Śāntipa and Kāmadhenu] as teaching the threefold master division. [As for the level of consecration and the amount of teaching or instruction you get before treating somebody as a master], the three—the consecration and so forth—do not have to be in the two higher tantra sets. This is also the same for the lower sets. And you should not calculate the amount of tantric teaching and instructions [443] in terms of a complete or incomplete teaching of a tantra, or of a chapter and so on of it, but rather take it as being any teaching, from a single verse on the topic of the generation or completion stage and so forth that is unique to tantra on up, because the earlier extract about taking just a single verse is [said] in the context of the master relative to whom the root downfall is incurred. And also because Śāntipa, in his *Handful of Flowers Commentary* on the fifth section of the *Guhyasamāja Tantra*'s[84] "Those who disparage the master from the heart..." explains, "Whoever taught them a perfect mantra or meditative stabilization is also their master." Also, his *Jewel Lamp Commentary* on the *Black Yamāri Tantra* says this in the context of teaching the root downfall. Nagpopa [in his *Lamp to View the Path*] says that in this context, the masters may be those who have all three [qualities] of having explained a tantra and so forth, those who have two, or those who have any one of these [qualities]. The production of a root downfall is the same; only the gravity differs.

The Action That Causes the Downfall

"Disparaging" those "masters" is a root downfall. To what extent? [Śāntipa] in his *Jewel Lamp Commentary* on the *Black Yamāri Tantra,* "As [the *Black Yamāri Tantra*] says, 'Vajra masters are those who bestow consecration. Being impolite to us is getting heated and ridiculing us.'" So forsake that.[85] If you do not forsake [that], it is a root downfall. [The *Guhyasamāja Tantra*] says, "Those who disparage the master from the heart accomplish nothing even after they have practiced." To "disparage the master from the heart" is to disparage those from whom you have received advice on the precepts and so forth [thinking,] [444] "Now what use is there in listening to their advice, and so on?"

So, "Even if a guru who teaches you the maṇḍala behaves badly, physically or mentally, understanding [the consequences], never disparage."

The earlier extract [from the *Black Yamāri Tantra*] explains the mode of disparaging that leads to the root downfall of forsaking a master through being impolite and ridiculing, and the later part of the extract elaborates on that. Take it in this way because this is what Kāmadhenu also says when explaining that you should not disparage a performance tantra master. The earlier extract thus cited is in the *Ornament of Kosala,* the latter in [Candrakīrti's] *Illuminating Lamp Commentary* on the fifth section of the *Guhyasamāja Tantra,* and Kāmadhenu cites the "Even if a guru..." passage from the *Susiddhi Tantra.*

So it says that at issue is not the amount of qualities possessed by masters who have been kind enough to teach us the Vajrayāna, but their connection with tantric doctrine. That is the reason we have to consider them the highest field of worship, and revere them as our gurus with body, speech, and mind. Shrugging this off [with the thought] "There is nothing in this," is disparaging or abusing to the extent that leads to the full root downfall. Since the *Ornament of the Vajra Essence Tantra* also says "disparage the master from the heart" in the context of naming the first root downfall, even though there are a number of different positions about the extent of the disparaging that leads to the first root downfall, the position taken by these two masters [Śāntipa and Kāmadhenu] is best.

Śāntipa, in [the passage just cited from] his *Jewel Lamp Commentary* says there has to be the *Guhyasamāja Tantra*'s "disparaging the master from the heart" for it to be the first root downfall, and in his *Handful of Flowers Commentary* on the *Guhyasamāja Tantra* he says, "To 'disparage the master from the heart' is to [445] disparage the master repeatedly, to like doing so, to feel no regret, and not to repair the fault in accord with doctrine."

Thus he says all of these—repeated disparaging and so forth—are necessary, so all must be present for a root downfall. These are equivalent to the [four] factors of greater involvement necessary for a root downfall in bodhisattva ordination. Citing the *Ākāśagarbha Sūtra,* Ānandagarbha and Śāntipa, in the context of establishing that rejecting the doctrines of the three vehicles is a root downfall in tantra, say the factors of greater involvement must be present for a root downfall, so, by extension, this is the case for other root downfalls as well.

"Repeatedly" means without break—you did it earlier and you have not stopped wanting to do it again. "To like" means to feel glad about it in your heart. "To feel no regret" is [the *Bodhisattva Levels*'] "to see a value in it," or to see no fault in it. "Not to repair the fault" means to attach no importance, out of a sense of shame or embarrassment, to the fault. I have already ascertained what these are in my *Explanation* of the morality chapter of the *Bodhisattva Levels,*[86] [where I have said that "non-production of conscience and lack of concern for the disadvantages" are the two absences, and "desire to do it in future and being pleased with and glad of it" are the two presences necessary for greater involvement]. These [two] absences, furthermore, must be absences from the second instant after the motivation of the downfall up to the moment right before the completion of the actual deed, and the [two] presences must be present during that period as well. If there is a lack of any one of the absences or presences, there is no defeat. And since [Śāntipa] says [446] they are necessary for the first root downfall, with the exception of the [fifth]—giving up bodhicitta—logically they are applicable to all the other downfalls too. Je Rinpoche Go [Khugpa Lhache] meant something similar when he said in his *Guhyasamāja Panacea,*[87] "There is a defeat if, when setting about it, you have no shame, when doing the actual deed you do not apply the antidote, and if, afterwards, you have no regret."

The *Red* and *Black Yamāri Tantras* and the *Clusters of Quintessential Instructions* give the name [of the first root downfall] just as it is in this text. In the *Vajra Tent Tantra* and [Vimalagupta's] *Ornament of the Guhyasamāja Tantra,* "disparaging the master" occurs [without the qualification "from the heart"]. They mean the same thing, however.

The *Commentary on the Root Downfalls* [attributed to Mañjuśrīkīrti] says[88] that in the case in which a master parts from life, if later confessed before the expiry of the term [your life], it is a root downfall. If you expire [before confession] it is a defeat,[89] and in the case in which [the master] does not part from life it is a gross defeat. Such an assertion, that even though the master has died there is no defeat, and that a root downfall and a defeat are different, is preposterous. The *Commentary on Difficult Points to Do with Root Downfalls*[90] also mentions many ways of becoming a root downfall, but they are clearly untenable, so, fearing prolixity I desist from a detailed discussion.

The Reason Disparaging the Master in That Fashion Causes a Downfall

The reason that disparaging them causes a root downfall is "since the vajra holder," Vajradhara, "said that" any of the two "siddhis" established in the disciple's mindstream "flow" only "from" pleasing "the masters." That a downfall of that type is the first root downfall "is said" in the tantras.

A Downfall in Which All the Parts Are Not Complete

Disparaging and belittling the object, the master, to an extent that does not amount to the root downfall is not a root downfall since the parts are not complete, but it falls within the category of a defeat, [447] just as, for example, in the context of bodhisattva ordination, small and middling outflows fall within the defeat category, and, in the prātimokṣa context, gross and minor offenses connected with the categories of defeat and [the categories of offenses] still allowing one to remain in the order[91] fall within those categories, respectively.

Even though some explanations of the root downfalls say these are [a separate category of] minor offenses, still, take the category as above, since there are exclusively defeats and gross downfalls, and they are not the latter. Know that these are also [found among the downfalls discussed] below.

While it is possible, as taught earlier, to commit [one of the five] heinous crimes or reject the doctrine and still set out through the door of the Vajrayāna, practice, and get the supreme siddhi, those who disparage the master from the heart accomplish nothing even after they have practiced. The *Guhyasamāja Tantra* thus says this is worse than even a heinous crime. So of all the root downfalls, be particularly careful not to be guilty of this one. Furthermore, even though you can prevent rebirth in a state of woe by means of confession and proper restoration [of the pledge], still your attainment of siddhis recedes far into the distance.

It is true that belittling those who give the two [prātimokṣa and bodhisattva] ordinations of the Definitions Vehicle, and belittling those lamas who explain the pure path of emptiness and compassion are not among the root downfalls, but they are still extremely grave faults. Nevertheless, there is a difference between the size of a downfall (a variable of the promise given), and the weight of an offense (posited relative to the field [victim] and relative intensity of motivation). You should, therefore, be extremely careful about these as well. And while it is true [448] that [Mañjuśrīkīrti] in his *Ornament for the Essence,* as well as Nagpopa, say the following about what are analogous to and semblances of faults, "Here, know the immorality of rejecting the master and so forth to be heavy, light, corrected, and resembling,"[92] still these are nothing other than downfalls with incomplete parts.

Second Root Downfall

> They say the second downfall is to overstep the words of the sugatas. [Mā 3ab]

This has two parts. The *object [relative to which the downfall is incurred]* is the words of the sugatas.[93] [Dharmakīrti's] *Commentary on the "Compendium of Valid Cognitions"* says, "Those with three cause-eliminating qualities are sugatas." Thus they are "sugatas," that is, buddhas, because they go well or beautifully (since they give no basis for suffering), because they are gone without return (since for them the [power of] the seed of the view of self is exhausted), and because they are totally gone (since everything to be eliminated has ended). Nagpopa [in his *Lamp to View the Path*] says their "words" are the three vehicles.

The action that causes the downfall is "to overstep" their words. As for the way you overstep, since Nagpopa says not overstepping their words is practicing all the training advice of the three vows together as noncontradictory, on an ascending scale, he is asserting that it is overstepping those. If you take this as simply breaking a promise [to keep a vow] of the Buddha, then every downfall would have to be this second root downfall, so he is not asserting that. Śāntipa [in his *Jewel Lamp Commentary*] says overstepping their words is willfully ignoring their words. So, combining the ideas of the two commentaries together, three factors are operative in this: [1] vis-à-vis a promise to keep any of the three vows preached by the buddhas, [2] knowingly breaking it, [449] and [3] being motivated by the wish to willfully ignore it.

The other commentaries are all in disagreement about what the words are and about how you overstep them, and [Mañjuśrīkīrti in his] *Commentary on the Root Downfalls* in particular says that there are no defeats in this downfall. Many indeed are the apparently clear passages from the tantras cited in [these different interpretations of] overstepping the orders. Since none instill a feeling of confidence I do not write about them.

One Tibetan lama[94] says that the eight defeats in the *Bodhisattva Levels* and the four prātimokṣa defeats are the root downfall of overstepping their words. This is not in any Indian scripture, nor is it tenable, because you are never, in any of the three vow systems, given permission to incur a root downfall relative to that ordination, yet there are times when you are permitted to murder and so forth within this [tantric] ordination [though to do so would constitute a root downfall in the prātimokṣa or bodhisattva system].

The tantras "say" this sort of downfall is "the second downfall." The *Red* and *Black Yamāri Tantras*, the *Vajra Tent Tantra*, the *Ornament of the Vajra Essence Tantra*, the *Ornament of the Guhyasamāja Tantra*, and the *Clusters of Quintessential Instructions* set out the downfall of overstepping the words of the sugatas in harmony with that. Willfully ignoring doctrine other than the promises of the three vows and unknowingly ignoring [promises] are downfalls with incomplete parts. Connect this with [the downfalls discussed] below also, where the context allows.

Third Root Downfall

> The third is displaying cruelty to vajra relatives out of anger. [Mā 3cd]

This has two parts. The *object* is those who have become "relatives" by way of the "Vajra" Vehicle because of having the same birth place. Nagpo Damtsigdorje says about them:

> Close vajra relatives get pledges from the same master, maṇḍala, knowledge man, or knowledge woman. Distant [450] vajra relatives get them separately, that is, different ones from different ones. All who have set out in the Mahāyāna are kin. The root downfall is posited relative to the first two, and [a fault] concordant in part [with that downfall] relative to the other.

The *Ornament of Kosala*, however, says:

> "Not being unfriendly to a vajra relative." "Not being unfriendly" [means] not getting angry at each other—at those who have entered a maṇḍala through the same master.

Also Śāntipa [in his *Jewel Lamp Commentary*]:

> "Relatives" are those who have received consecration in a maṇḍala from the same master. Do not, out of envy and so forth, display their faults.

Thus they say the same master is needed, which is sensible, because were the guru to be different, the birth place would be different, and the meaning of "relative" would be lost. Furthermore, although it is true that there are three relatives who have listened and so on [i.e., who are relatives based on a master consecrating them, teaching them a tantra, or giving them instructions, as in the *Black Yamāri Tantra* (442.3)], here they are consecration relatives as in the extracts [from the *Ornament of Kosala* and *Jewel Lamp Commentary* just] cited, and it is sufficient if their consecration is into a tantra from the lower two sets. Lakṣmīṅkara [in his *Root Downfalls Commentary*] asserts that they should have received a shared consecration and pledges in the same maṇḍala, and that their practice should be a shared one. This would lead to a more serious infraction. It is not necessary however that those [tantric practitioners who might incur this downfall] receive them at the same time and in the same maṇḍala to produce the root downfall.

The *Stainless Light Commentary* says, "It is if they get infuriated at a vajra relative, old or young, who is in training." Thus it says they have vows. Since, contextually, the vows here have to be mantric vows, and since that [what is necessary in the *Kālacakra Tantra*] is also similar to this [what is necessary in the set of non-*Kālacakra* tantras], they have to have mantric vows.

The "sister" set out separately from "relative" in the *Cleansing All States of Woe Tantra* where it says, "Practitioners should not disparage vajra relatives, sisters, and vajra women," [451] is included within relatives. She is a relative as explained in the *Illumination of the "Compendium of Principles,"* in which it says that relatives are those who have entered a maṇḍala with the same master.

The action that causes the downfall is "displaying cruelty" or picking out faults "out of anger," or having got upset. Here the *Root Downfall Commentary Amṛtacandra* and Lakṣmīṅkara['s *Root Downfalls Commentary*] say the one over there has to know [you are] a relative, and the latter also says you are cognizant of the fact that [the one over there] is a relative. These are also necessary here [for the complete downfall].

[Mañjuśrīkīrti in his] *Commentary on the Root Downfalls* says the downfall is primarily incurred not by body and speech, but by an angry mind, and he does not take "displaying cruelty" as voicing faults. Some Tibetans explain in that way as well, but they are wrong, because both the *Red* and *Black Yamāri Tantras* say, "Similarly, do not get angry at a relative and proclaim something cruel." Śrīdhara's two [*Red* and *Black Yamāri*] *Maṇḍala Rituals* also say, "Similarly, do not out of anger say something cruel about one of your relatives." Both [Śāntipa's and Nagpopa's] commentaries on the *Black Yamāri Tantra* explain like this also. Moreover, the *Ornament of the Vajra Essence Tantra* says, "Shouting down[95] a relative out of hatred," as do the *Clusters of Quintessential Instructions* and the *Ornament of the Guhyasamāja Tantra*. Hence, even though in the *Vajra Tent Tantra* we find "...hatred for a relative...," it has to be taken in the same way. And even if you accept the reading *rdo rje sbun la 'khro ba ni* [in place of *rdo rje sbun la 'khro nas ni* "...to a vajra relative out of anger"] found in some editions, you still have to read *'khro ba* [anger] as an instrumental *khro bas* [because of anger].

To sum up—when there is [1] a vajra relative consecrated by the same guru [2] who has mantric vows and [3] you are cognizant of the fact, if, [4] motivated by hatred, [452] you give voice to a cruelty and [5] [the relative] hears what you say and understands what you mean, the five factors are complete and it is the third root downfall.

Fourth Root Downfall

> The victors say the fourth is giving up love for living beings. [Mā 4ab]

This has two parts. The *object* is phrased in the plural "living beings," but it is any living being whatsoever.

The action that causes the downfall is "giving up love." Nagpopa:

> The Mahāyāna considers all living beings like an only child and never forsakes them. A Mahāyāna detached from the field of living beings, like a firefly given the name "possessing sunlight," is [a Mahāyāna] in name only.

And Śāntipa says, "Never give up the loving thought that wants a living being to achieve incomparable benefit and bliss."

Both their explanations are similar in meaning, so it is the opposite of that. Were giving it up the thought, "I am not able to bring about the happiness and benefit of living beings," this would become indistinguishable from the next [downfall], giving up bodhicitta. How, then, is it given up? Is it by getting angry at them, by not producing a special feeling of love for them, or through thinking "I hope they are not happy"? The *Red Yamāri Tantra* says, "Never give up loving thoughts for all living beings," and the *Ornament of the Vajra Essence Tantra* says, "Without loving thoughts you forsake living beings." Thus they say it is giving up loving thoughts, so take it to be producing the thought, "I hope [someone or some group] is unhappy." [453] To give up or not give up love is, therefore, according to these tantras, to give up or not give up loving thoughts. Hence the explanation in *Amṛtacandra* and by Lakṣmīṅkara that it is when you ignore a living being who is suffering even though you could help them and so forth is not what is meant. This [above explanation] is what is said to be giving up love in this [root] text, and likewise, the above extracts [from Nagpopa and so on] say something similar. Thus "the Victors say" that the fourth root downfall, giving up love, is when, taking any living being whatsoever as the object, you produce the thought, "I hope they are unhappy."

In the *Black Yamāri Tantra* this comes after disparaging tenet systems [i.e., after the sixth root downfall according to the order given in this text]. Nagpopa's explanation follows that. Śāntipa's explanation follows the order given here.

Fifth Root Downfall

> Fifth is giving up bodhicitta, the root of dharmas. [Mā 4cd]

This has two parts. The *object* is "bodhicitta," the solemn oath that you will attain buddhahood for the sake of living beings. The *Bounteous Array Sūtra* says of it, "Child of good family! Bodhicitta is the seed, as it were, of every Buddhadharma."Thus it is the root of all "dharmas" and good qualities of a "buddha."

Śāntipa calls bodhicitta the compassion that wants others to be free from misery and its cause. As one side of the solemn oath to attain buddhahood in order to free wandering beings from misery, this indicates the other [side, your future buddhahood, which is the means to accomplish this compassionate wish]. Hence, as Nagpopa says, take it to be the bodhicitta that is a prayer. As for the difference between this and love, Nagpopa says, "Love precedes and bodhicitta is the fundamental state [454] to which it leads."

The action that causes the downfall is if you give up that prayer bodhicitta, thinking, "I am not able to get enlightened for the sake of infinite living beings." That is the fifth root downfall. Since Nagpopa says *not* giving it up is swearing the solemn oath of that thought [of enlightenment] and not breaking it, giving it up is [thinking "I am not able..."]. Some commentaries on the root downfalls also say it is to give up the jasmine-like [fluid]. I will deal with that in the context of the *Kālacakra Tantra.*

With the exception of the *Vajra Tent Tantra,* the name given to this infraction is the same as in the above extracts. Since in this case just giving it up constitutes the root downfall, even if the parts are not complete, it is still a defeat.

Sixth Root Downfall

> Sixth is criticizing the doctrine of your own or other tenet systems. [Mā 5ab]

This has two parts. The *object:* Nagpopa construes "your own" as Buddhist, "other" as *tīrthika*[96] [i.e., non-Buddhist], and "doctrine" as the way to high rebirth, and cites, "If you criticize the tīrthikas it causes Vairocana to recede."

Still, although it is wrong to ridicule tīrthikas out of a wish to find fault with them, I feel uneasy saying they are the object based on which the root downfall is incurred. Let us, therefore, construe "your own system of tenets" as Mantra, and "other system of tenets" as the Perfection Vehicle, as in the *Commentary on Difficult Points to Do with Root Downfalls.* "Or" is to show that among the two objects of ridicule, either is enough [to cause the root downfall]. The *Clusters of Quintessential Instructions,* [Ratnarakṣita's] *Padminī Commentary on the Saṃvarodaya Tantra,* [Ratnakīrti's] *Ritual Evocation of the One Who Owns the Entire Doctrine,* and the *Ornament of the Guhyasamāja Tantra* say, [455] "Criticizing the three vehicles..." What they intend by designating it thus is similar. In the *Red* and *Black Yamāri Tantras* again the meaning is similar, and the *Ornament of the Vajra Essence Tantra* says clearly, "Criticizing your own and other systems of tenets."

It seems the *Vajra Tent Tantra*'s, "Do not get repulsed by[97] the doctrines of others" is teaching one part [of the object only].

The action that causes the downfall is if you "criticize" or get repulsed by "the doctrines," those two sacred words [of a buddha—the Mantra and Perfection Vehicles]. As for the mode of criticism, Nagpopa does not explain clearly [in his *Lamp to View the Path*], while [Śāntipa in his] *Commentary to [Dīpaṃkarabhadra's] Guhyasamāja Maṇḍala Ritual* says, "Do not reject."

As the *Ākāśagarbha Sūtra* says:

> Bodhisattvas who reject or set out to refute a Śrāvaka Vehicle exegesis, a Pratyekabuddha Vehicle exegesis, or a Mahāyāna doctrine exegesis incur the second root downfall.

He thus establishes that rejecting a doctrine of the three vehicles is a root downfall. In the passage cited earlier [386.2] Ānandagarbha also says this. So, based on the sacred word of any of the three vehicles, [the action that causes the downfall] is deprecating it from the bottom of your heart with the thought, "The Buddha never said that." In regard to forsaking the Mahāyāna, Ārya Asaṅga [in the *Bodhisattva Levels*] has said that all the aforementioned parts must be complete, otherwise a defeat does not occur.

Question: Śāntipa in his *Jewel Lamp Commentary on the Black Yamāri Tantra* says:

> "Do not criticize," do not repulse [i.e., refute] with argument, because [456] wandering beings are gradually captivated and enlightened just by means of the vehicles they incline to. Opposing their inclination with violent arguments simply causes them to get angry, so leave it.

Thus he says that to criticize is to repulse [i.e., attempt to destroy] belief in a tenet system by argument. How does that [square with the interpretation given above? In response we say] there is no problem, because he is saying that when you have found fault with the Mantra or Perfection Vehicle and are repulsed, thinking, "These are not the sacred words [of the Buddha]," the inclination to believe in those two tenet systems stops as well. It is difficult for people new to a spiritual practice to feel admiration for the entire revelation [of the Buddha], but as it says in the *Bodhisattva Levels,* there is no fault in not believing in a particular doctrine of the Buddha so long as it is not actively denied as such.[98] The *Little Saṃvara Tantra* also says:

> They teach various ways of life for living beings with many different interests. They teach various methods for those to be tamed in a variety of ways. Even if you do not admire it when they teach a profound doctrine, do not criticize, but remember that the true nature of dharmas is inconceivable. Since it is not an object for me, I do not understand the true nature of dharmas that the *mahātmas*—the *sambuddhas* and their offspring—understand.

The *Ornament for the Mahāyāna Sūtras* and [Nāgārjuna in his] *Precious Garland of Advice for the King* also say there is no fault if you simply let it be.[99] This really is a vital insight.

Rejecting a doctrine of the three vehicles, then, is the "sixth" root downfall.

Seventh Root Downfall

> Seventh is speaking publicly about secrets to immature beings. [Mā 5cd]

This has two parts. The *object* is similar to these [i.e., is immature beings] in the *Red* and *Black Yamāri Tantras,* the *Clusters of Quintessential Instructions,* and the *Ornament of the Guhyasamāja Tantra.* [457] The *Ornament of the Vajra Essence Tantra* says, "...disclosing secrets to those who are unsuitable receptacles...," and the *Vajra Tent Tantra* says, "Do not talk about suchness to the unlucky." These are saying that "immature beings" are those whose mindstreams have not been made into suitable receptacles for tantra through consecration, and are therefore "unlucky." So, as the *Commentary on Difficult Points to Do with Root Downfalls* and the *Root Downfall Commentary Amṛtacandra* say, this refers to those in whom no faith arises when the secrets are proclaimed.

Nagpopa describes five types of immaturity: those with base cravings are immature as receptacles, those without the vase consecration are ritually immature, those without the secret and transcendental wisdom consecrations are still not completely ritually mature, those who have incurred a root downfall and not restored it have regressed into immaturity, and those without the suchness of the fourth consecration are immature in the sense that they fear the profound. He does not, however, say clearly that they are the object of the downfall. Śāntipa says, "...those who are untutored, who have not gathered wisdom..." [referring to] those who understand the topic but lack the wisdom to believe it.

The action that causes the downfall is "speaking publicly about secrets" [to them]. As for the secrets spoken about, Śāntipa says, "Here you should not make statements about 'secrets' to do with emptiness." This [refers] not just to emptiness, but to tantric secrets to do with emptiness. Nagpopa takes the secrets as the maṇḍala, just one pledge seal, just one pledge to do with secret terminology, a gathering of a tantric feast, and so forth, and knowledge [in which clear light and illusory body are] yoked together, and says [458] you should not disclose these. In short, it is the topic of the secret, true reality in mantra to do with the two [generation and completion] stages and so on. Take the *Vajra Tent Tantra*'s "[Do not talk about] suchness [to the unlucky]" like that too. Lakṣmīṅkara says the one over there has to understand the meaning, you have to be cognizant of the fact [that they are not a receptacle], and the special purpose must be absent—*purpose* meaning the great purpose of taming others.

A learned person [Dragpa Gyeltsen] says that revealing secret, material objects like the six ornaments, pictures of the body, sacred books, or the *cang de'u* [a woven connecting-piece between the two sides of the damaru drum] is a root downfall. This is not correct because the tantras and commentaries explain the fault in terms of proclaiming a secret doctrine into the ear, and do not say that revealing material objects to the eye is a fault.[100]

It is improper to reveal secrets unique to each progressively higher tantra set to those consecrated in a lower tantra set, and, similarly, it is improper to teach the unique secrets connected with the three higher consecrations to those who have only received a disciple or vase consecration. And it is absolutely improper to have someone generate themselves as the deity and so on and practice that, unless they have entered at least an action tantra maṇḍala and received at least the vase consecration. The first part of the *Compendium of Principles:*

> Do not speak with those who have not seen the great maṇḍala.
> It would mean you would be breaking your pledge.

And:

> Today Vajrasattva has perfectly entered your heart. If you talk about the practice he immediately is destroyed and gone.

Thus many scriptures stress not talking about the secrets by saying that the revealers break their pledges, and that the Vajrasattva who has entered their hearts departs, no longer resides there, and so on [459]. And since the *Vajraḍākinī Saṃvara Continuation Tantra* cited earlier [380.1] says that those who have not entered a maṇḍala accomplish nothing even after they have done the practice, even if those disciples were to practice, they would gain absolutely no special siddhis at all, so it is purposeless [to talk with them about the secrets of tantra]. Again, the third section of the *Buddhakapāla Tantra* says, "Just as a house without a child to carry on the line is emptied by mere death, so too, without consecration, all knowledge is empty." Just as a stringed instrument that is put together without strings cannot be played, so to, without consecration, there is no practice of mantras and concentrations. And the same text also says that both the revealer and the listener do something very wrong: "The unconsecrated fool who says, 'I bestow consecrations,' goes to hell along with the disciple for as long as the buddhas remain."

[Abhayākara's] *Fearless Footsteps* explains that they stay in hell right up until it is fully emptied. [Saraha's] *Commentary on the Difficult Points of the Buddhakapāla Tantra Called Jñānavatī* says these three verses are connected [specifically] to the three higher consecrations. It is only by way of illustration, however, that it does so, because the *Fearless Footsteps* says there is no doubt they apply to every consecration.

The second section of the *Yoginī Tantra Called An Ornamental Spot of Mahāmudrā* says, "Those who arrogantly explain a tantric text without consecration, master and disciple, go to a hell right after death even if they have attained siddhis." Thus it says that even if the master and disciple have attained some shared siddhis, both are reborn in a hell. [460] Hence you have to take the permission[101] for Acalaśuci and so forth as [permission] for no more than entrance into action tantra maṇḍalas, not above that, and the permission for Prabhāskarīprajñā and so on as permission for no more than entry into maṇḍalas. It is totally improper, without consecration and having just received permission, to practice these deities and so forth.

Thus, when there is [1] someone who has not been matured by consecration, [2] someone in whom no faith arises when the secrets are proclaimed, and [3] you are cognizant of the fact, if [4] you talk about an unshared secret and [5] it is understood while [6] there is no great purpose—[such as the purpose of] taming others—the six factors are complete and the seventh root downfall [is incurred].

As explained earlier [419–22], it is acceptable to give entry to a maṇḍala even without bestowing consecration. Because there is a special dispensation, you do not incur the fault of speaking publicly about secrets. There are a number of parallels to this in the Vinaya [where, for example, a special dispensation is given to sick monks and nuns to do what is otherwise forbidden].

If you impart a [nontantric Mahāyāna] Definitions Vehicle doctrine to one who is not a receptacle, it is not the root downfall, but there is a misdeed in which all the parts are not complete.

Eighth Root Downfall

> Eighth is treating the aggregates, which are in essence the five buddhas, with contempt. [Mā 6ab]

This has two parts. The *object* is said to be the five "aggregates" of forms, feelings, discriminations, karmic formations, and consciousnesses "that are in essence," or have as their nature, "the five buddhas," Vairocana, Ratnasaṃbhava, Amitābha, Amoghasiddhi, and Akṣobhya, respectively. Since the *Red* and *Black Yamāri Tantras* and the *Vajra Tent Tantra* say "your own aggregates," the object of this root downfall has to be your own aggregates.

The action that causes the downfall. "Treating" them [461] "with contempt" or despising them is the downfall. As for the way you treat them with contempt and despise them, Nagpopa takes the aggregates to be Vairocana and so forth on the strength of the buddhas operating through them as their nature, and because they develop into buddhas. He says that you should make inner fire oblations [to them] and do an enjoyable practice that takes it easy [on them]. He says that treating the aggregates with contempt means to put a stop to them, jump off cliffs, take demeaning vows specific to the propitiation of particular deities [that require you to go on all fours like an animal and so on], torture yourself, sever organs or limbs, fast, or do severe ascetic acts and austerities. Śāntipa says:

> Since by this mantric mode, through vigor, enlightenment resides in these very five aggregates, and since it says, "Those who despise [the aggregates] are carcasses ruining a person's happiness," they should not be despised. [The word "aggregate" renders the Sanskrit word *skandha,* which also means "shoulder."] Since these [aggregates] are for the load [they are called] *skandha.* [That is, before enlightenment they locate the burden of suffering life, and after enlightenment they carry all beings, in the sense that someone responsible for another's welfare is said to carry them.]

Through this, he explains despising. In short, when you hurt yourself by afflicting yourself with any of the methods of [religious] torture intended to injure your own aggregates, it is the eighth root downfall.

In the *Red* and *Black Yamāri Tantras* and in the *Vajra Tent Tantra* we find just "...despise the aggregates...," while in the *Ornament of the Vajra Essence Tantra,* the *Ornament of the Guhyasamāja Tantra,* the *Clusters of Quintessential Instructions,* and [Ratnarakṣita's] *Padminī Commentary on the Saṃvarodaya Tantra* it says, "...despise the aggregates that are in essence the jinas..." similar to this. The significance of the qualification "...that are in essence the five buddhas..." comes out in the *Padminī Commentary on the Saṃvarodaya Tantra* where it says:

> All seconds have been forsaken. Do not make a distinction between the five aggregates and the five tathāgatas.

So I think there may be two doors leading to the root downfall. [462] One way is to despise the aggregates by making a distinction, thinking, "You should not habituate yourself to the idea that the five aggregates are the five tathāgatas," the reason being that these two are unclean and clean, respectively. The second way is to despise the aggregates as taught above.

The *Commentary on Difficult Points to do with Root Downfalls* says suicide by poison and so forth is the root downfall, and preparing for that is the misdeed. This is an egregious error, because if you have died there is no basis [the body] for the downfall to happen. This [commentary] does not, therefore, appear to be have been written by Aśvaghoṣa.

Although [Mañjuśrīkīrti in his] *Commentary on the Root Downfalls* explains that the close mindfulness meditation on the uncleanliness of the body is the root downfall, and although there are others as well who similarly say that taking the body to be suffering and unclean is the root downfall, they are wrong. The mantra scriptures talk about many meditations on suffering and uncleanliness. The *Vajra Tip Tantra* says to meditate on uncleanliness: "Those with a longing for sex should remove it by meditation on ugliness." And [Āryadeva's] *Lamp Uniting One to the Practice* says:

> Through these stages they should set forth into the spiritual practice completely free of elaboration. Its stages are as follows. Among them, at the very first, practitioners recollect the sufferings of a saṃsāra that has no beginning. Longing for the happiness that is nirvāṇa, they should take up[102] all the hectic activities. Finally they should cultivate the notion that even the power to rule over a kingdom is suffering.

Ninth Root Downfall

> Ninth is entertaining doubts about the essential purity of dharmas. [Mā 6cd]

This has two parts. [463] The *object* is "the essential purity of dharmas," the emptiness that is the lack of own-being, the absence of elaboration. [Abhayākara's] *Clusters Concerning Vajrayāna Downfalls*[103] says, "Doubting the purity that is the lack of own-being in dharmas." And Śāntipa [in his *Jewel Lamp Commentary*]:

> "Essenceless dharmas," the perfection of wisdom. Never despise it, because:

> The unintelligent hear this and reject it. Having rejected it, they have no refuge and go to Avīci [hell].

The *Ornament of the Vajra Essence Tantra* designates it as it is here. The *Black Yamāri Tantra* says [in Tibetan translation] *Grong pa'i chos ni sun mi gdon* ["Town dharmas not expel repulsion"[104]] and Nagpopa's *Lamp to View the Path* has something similar, but throws no light on it. Śrīdhara's *Black Yamāri Maṇḍala Ritual* also says, "Do not reject the dharmas of saṃsāra." Nevertheless, since Śāntipa reads, [as cited above,] "'Essenceless dharmas'...never despise," and some editions of Śrīdhara's *Red Yamāri Maṇḍala Ritual* read [in Tibetan translation] *Ngo bo'i chos rnams sun mi dbyung* ["Essential dharmas not repulsed"], take the *Red Yamāri Tantra* statement [in Tibetan translation] *Bcom ldan chos ni sun mi dbyung* ["Lord dharmas not repulsed"] as does Śāntipa, [and construe it to mean "essenceless"]. Construe the meaning of the *Ornament of the Guhyasamāja Tantra*'s, "Doubting the purity of the holy dharmas...," and Bhavyakīrti's statement, "...entertaining doubts about the Mahāyāna..." in his *Commentary on the Difficult Points of the Saṃvarodaya Tantra Pleasing to the Heroic Ones* as above.

The action that causes the downfall is "entertaining doubts about" not believing in and rejecting that, because the *Red* and *Black Yamāri Tantras* [464] say repulsion [i.e., refuting]. Thus not believing profound emptiness and rejecting it is the ninth root downfall.

Although Nagpopa explains this in detail and says it is teaching definitive meaning to the philosophically unsophisticated holders of [Buddhist] positions requiring interpretation, causing the minds of others to get repulsed and go wrong, [an explanation] like Śāntipa's is best.

Tenth Root Downfall

> Tenth is held to persistently show affection to the wicked. [Mā 7ab]

This has two parts. The *object* is "wicked" living beings who despise the Three Jewels and the lama, who wipe out the doctrine and so forth, and against whom violent means have to be employed. The *Cleansing All States of Woe Tantra* says, "The wise must steel themselves and kill scoundrels who despise the Three Jewels, damage the Buddhadharma, and actively despise the guru."

The action that causes the downfall is to treat them as friends and physically "show affection" or voice it. They say that even when you have to use violence against these kinds of people, still you must produce great compassion, so loving them in your mind is not included in the downfall. Both [Nagpopa and Śāntipa's] commentaries understand it as I have explained above. They teach that it is a downfall when you treat them as friends, not that it is a root downfall when you fail to use violence against them. Question: But what about the *Six-Face Yamāri Tantra* that says, "Wise practitioners who want to help living beings do not murder," and then goes on to say:

> Oppose the wicked. Do it openly, or with a spell, magical weapon, meditative concentration, or poison. Those who do not do so definitely [465] break their pledge.

[In response we say] this teaches that those with great compassion who can cause [the victims to take] rebirth in a buddha's pure land and so forth, can revivify corpses with [other] consciousnesses, and who have direct knowledge of all their previous and future lives, must, in order to prevent them from having to experience interminable suffering in a state of woe, employ violence when they cannot find any other method to stop them doing what should not be done. Not only is there no fault attached to others not employing violence, were they to do so it would be a terrible crime. The *Padminī Commentary on the Saṃvarodaya Tantra* says:

> These activities are only for yogis who are able to transfer [consciousness] out of a body and cause the person to take birth in heaven or a pure buddha field, or who are able to reintroduce consciousness [and revivify a corpse]. If they put up barriers, but still those despoiling the Three Jewels do not stop, then praying to the buddhas and bodhisattvas for knowledge, and generating an intense feeling of pity, they proceed to do the [violent] practice as explained.

You can know the pledge for a specific number of murders and so forth from the long explanation in the *Stainless Light Commentary* [on the *Kālacakra Tantra*]. Again, though, the *Mañjuśrī Root Tantra* says that even [the Mauryan emperor Candragupta's minister] Cāṇakya, who was an adept in Yamāntaka practice, was born in hell after he died because of employing violence. Therefore, it goes without saying that the same will hold true for others as well.

> A Brahmin child known widely as Cāṇakya [466] practiced Krodha, and that evil-minded person practiced Yamāntaka as well. He was overtaken by rage and destroyed the livelihood of many living beings. For three reigns he committed many atrocities. He was an evil brahmin who lived for a very long time. Through the power of his mantras he caused an opponent of the gods to resort to his body [i.e., became possessed by an evil spirit], and after the opponent of the gods had entered his body, he lived for a long time. Then, when even that body perished, he went to Avīci hell.

It goes on to say that after he died there he took birth again as an evil dragon and then was born as the king of the hungry ghosts with great miraculous powers. It ends by saying:

> Therefore those who practice mantra do not engage in violence. The buddhas and bodhisattvas forbid violence. The supremely compassionate buddhas and bodhisattvas who have great supernatural abilities reveal all the activities in order to reveal the power of mantra.

Therefore, except in the case of the three ameliorating circumstances [present in amazing persons], such violent acts are generally forbidden. They are simply mentioned in mantra. Consider them wrong and do not do them.

The *Red* and *Black Yamāri Tantras,* the *Ornament of the Vajra Essence Tantra,* and the *Clusters of Quintessential Instructions* say the downfall arises from having shown affection to the wicked, just as it is explained in this text. The *Padminī Commentary on the Saṃvarodaya Tantra* also mentions a particular length of time for the show of affection: "...affectionate toward the wicked at the start, middle, and end." The *Ornament of the Guhyasamāja Tantra* says the downfall arises from "...being without affection and joy for anger," [467] and the *Commentary* on this text [the *Vajra Vehicle Root Downfalls*] said to be by Jowo [Atiśa] has something similar, but you should take the earlier meaning.

The words of the root text in the *Root Downfall Commentary Amṛtacandra* and Lakṣmīṅkara's *Commentary* do not agree with this [text]. Still [we do not need to question the reading on that account, because] those are not commentaries on this text.[105]

Eleventh Root Downfall

> Eleventh is the false imagination of dharmas without names and so forth. [Mā 7cd]

This has two parts. The *object* is "dharmas" ultimately "without" all the conceptuality set forth through "names" (the "and so forth" brings in phrases and sentences). [Abhayākara's] *Clusters Concerning Vajrayāna Downfalls* says, "False imagination of a start, middle, and end of all dharmas that are empty of a start, middle, and end," when identifying the eleventh, and the *Padminī Commentary on the Saṃvarodaya Tantra* says, in the context of this eleventh:

> Free from all false imagination. Without falsely imagining a start and so forth, where there is emptiness at the start, middle, and end of dharmas.

And:

> False imagination where there is this or that emptiness...

Also, the *Ornament of the Vajra Essence Tantra* says, "False imagination about what is inexorably empty." It means false imagination about the inexorably empty, about dharmas that are simply empty of own-being.

The action that causes the downfall is "false imagination of" a particular sign—a name and so forth for those dharmas. This is the opinion of the *Clusters of Quintessential Instructions,* the *Ritual Evocation of the One Who Owns the Entire Doctrine,* and the *Padminī Commentary on the Saṃvarodaya Tantra.*

Question: If, relative to dharmas, you should not produce the belief in a self of dharmas powered by beginningless residual impressions, [468] it would be an impossible practice; if you take [what you should not produce] as the superimposition of a truth powered by a philosophy, this would be indistinguishable from the ninth [downfall]—being repulsed by and rejecting the selflessness of dharmas. If the ninth is the downfall of denying that the teaching of emptiness is the sacred word of the Buddha, it would become the sixth. [How do you resolve this? In response we say that] here the downfall occurs when you attain the view of the selflessness of dharmas, and then, though you should resort to it continually, you do not do so. As Jñānaśrī says in his *Exclusion of the Two Vajrayāna Extremes:*

> The heart practice of mantric practitioners is, at all times, and on all occasions, viewing all dharmas as selfless, like illusions. As it says, "There is no need to talk at length. The reality in Mantrayāna is that whatever the yogis apprehend, they see it all as illusory."

Hence, viewing defilement and purification dharmas like illusions, these [yogis] eliminate afflictions without difficulty and avoid being conceited and so on about the wholesome. Since, just by that, they attain all of their extraordinary excellences, they keep it in their heart and obtain all good qualities. Thus he says you must not be without the view for any length of time. Still, he teaches that this is different from being a follower of the Middle Way school. After that he says:

> Objection: The assertion of the followers of the Middle Way school is also exactly like that. They say, "We have no conceit that 'I am in a state of absorption,' that 'I have gotten up [out of that state].'"

And:

> The victors said that making wholesome dharmas into a basis is like eating good food mixed with poison. [469]

Thus they say that at all times, and on all occasions, they view all defilement and purification dharmas like illusions, and not as anything different from that.

[Response]: This is true. Nevertheless, on that path there is no presentation of them breaking a vow when they do not view like that, based on its being a vow. [There are no vows], they are [just] without the misdeeds that occur on rare occasions because of extreme fatigue. On this [Vajrayāna] path it goes against a body, speech, and mind pledge. Since being without that understanding is presented as breaking a mind pledge, these [mantric practitioners] worry about that and it motivates them to never lose meditative stabilization. When they find themselves without it, they honestly restrain themselves and face up to the fact [that they have broken a vow], reapply themselves, and never lose it. Thus, just as the mind of the Tathāgata never grasps at things, so too the mind of the mantric practitioner is ever free from grasping at things. Like illusions, self and other are the same and not divisible. This is a Vajrayāna. It is a speedier, different path.[106] Hence this Mahāyāna is based on the person with sharp faculties.

Here, if [to keep this vow] you could never break the continuum of an understanding of emptiness, [it would be so hard that] it would be absurd, so it is not that. You have [to break the continuum of] a wish, of esteeming the view highly, [i.e., the downfall arises from not caring and from not esteeming the view highly]. In the absence of that [unbroken continuum of understanding], there is indeed a misdeed damaging the pledge, but not the root downfall.

Hence the measure of what constitutes a root downfall does not seem to be found other than in the *Commentary* said to be by Jowo [Atiśa]:

> "Dharmas without names, and so forth," or clear light and unity. [470] "False imagination," or falsely imagining them as something else inconsistent with those two natures, for a day and a night.

I think that perhaps this is best.

So, if those with tantric vows who are smart enough to understand emptiness when they study do not strive for the view of the selflessness of dharmas, it is not a root downfall, but there is clearly a misdeed. If they have found the view, then, as above, take it [as the root downfall]. To do otherwise, and to proffer the advice that the root downfall is when someone—anyone, regardless of whether they comprehend the view—with tantric vows, fails to keep the view that cuts grasping at signs is absurd. Does it have to be the Middle Way view, or is the Mind Only view sufficient? As the glorious Vāgīśvarakīrti says in his *Exposition of "Reality Shining like a Jewel,"* "The Consciousness Only and Middle Way texts are primary in the Mantra system too." Thus it can be either the Middle Way or Mind Only view. Since in Āryadeśa [India] there were many fully qualified tantric masters holding the Mind Only view, construe the ninth root downfall also as being repulsed by, in general, just the selflessness of dharmas. Do not take it as the Mind Only and Middle Way repulsion to each other's tenet system.

The statement in the *Ornament of the Guhyasamāja Tantra* about this root downfall, "...by superimposing the two extremes onto dharmas..." agrees with the above. The *Red* and *Black Yamāri Tantras* say, "...measuring out a limit for dharmas..." This is also found in the *Vajra Tent Tantra*. Śāntipa says it is [471] setting forth into concealing [i.e., conventional] dharmas that have been spoken about, without scriptures and preceptual advice, relying on just personal reasoning.[107] Nagpopa says that where the topic is the realization dharma that knows its own real mark—the wisdom without any name, without sentence or word, without symbol, and without expression—it is arguing about what it is or is not, falsely imagining that it does or does not exist, or, led by other texts and reasoning, entertaining doubt about it. Still, since Abhayākara, Vimalagupta, Ratnarakṣita, and many others have explained the thought of the master who composed this [root] text summarizing the meaning of those tantras as above, I take its interpretation of this as authoritative.

Thus if you have the view of the selflessness of dharmas and do not guard it, and a full day passes, it is the eleventh root downfall.

Twelfth Root Downfall

> Twelfth is said to be repulsing the minds of living beings who have faith. [Mā 8ab]

This has two parts. The *object* is similar to this in the *Red and Black Yamāri Tantras*, the *Ornament of the Vajra Essence Tantra*, the *Ornament of the Guhyasamāja Tantra*, and the *Clusters of Quintessential Instructions*. The *Vajra Tent Tantra* has "...of a fortunate living being...," so [the object] is "living beings who have faith" and are suitable receptacles for the path. As for what constitutes faith, Nagpopa does not say, but Śāntipa says, "Living beings who have faith," who trust in the share-object given by their father..."

Thus it is faith in the guiding instructions that the guru apportions out to the disciples. Contextually, this should be taken as instructions about the path of the supreme [Vajra]yāna.

The action that causes the downfall is [472] similar to this in the *Ornament of the Vajra Essence Tantra,* the *Vajra Tent Tantra,* the *Ornament of the Guhyasamāja Tantra,* the *Clusters of Quintessential Instructions,* and the *Padminī Commentary on the Saṃvarodaya Tantra.* The *Red* and *Black Yamāri Tantra*s say that it is deceiving those living beings, and Nagpopa takes it to be this as well. Śāntipa reads, "...arrest living beings who have faith..." but he does not explain how their thought is arrested. Still, it is if, with a willful intention to arrest their desire-to-do, you cause a mental repulsion. For this, do they have to stop the desire-to-do or not? The *Stream of Ambrosia Commentary,*[108] the *Root Downfall Commentary Amṛtacandra,* and [Mañjuśrīkīrti in his] *Commentary on the Root Downfalls* all explain based on stopping it, so it seems for the root downfall [the desire-to-do] has to stop.

Nagpopa mentions cheating on weights and measures and so on, deceiving with illusions and magical machines, and deceiving by teaching perverted doctrines and so forth, but does not clearly explain which of these is the root downfall. Still, Śāntipa, in line with this [root] text, says that the *Black Yamāri Tantra* intends arresting their thought, and a very large number of learned ones seem [to agree], so apparently it is best to construe the root downfall in terms of mental repulsion. Thus, when there is [1] a living being who is a suitable receptacle for Mahāyāna who has faith in a particular supreme [Vajra]yāna guiding instruction, and [2] with a willful intention to arrest their desire-to-do, you [3] employ some means to cause mental repulsion, and [4] their desire-to-do stops, it is the twelfth root downfall.

Although the *Commentary on Difficult Points to Do with Root Downfalls* and so forth say teaching perverted doctrines to those who have faith is what constitutes it, since that is said to be a gross, [and not a root,] downfall, it is not contextually appropriate.

Thirteenth Root Downfall

> Thirteenth is not resorting to pledges [473] as they are found.[109]
> [Mā 8cd]

This has two parts: how the root downfall happens in highest yoga tantra and how it happens in yoga tantra.

The Downfall in Highest Yoga Tantra

This has two parts. The *object* is your "pledges." Although, generally speaking, there are two pledges relating to food and protection, here, as Dārikapa says [in his *Vajra Verses Explaining the Kālacakra Consecration*], take them to be pledges relating to food and enjoyment. Śāntipa's explanation that it is not enjoying the blessed, five-nectar substances just indicates one part [of the whole object].

The action that causes the downfall is "not resorting to" those pledge substances just "as" they are. What sort of substances? Those "found" or gained from donations made by those who have pledges. At a properly convened tantric feast, or an all-male or all-female ritual party, when the excellent food and drink substances such as the five nectars are donated, it is thinking or suspecting that they are dirty and not accepting them. [Mañjuśrīkīrti's] *Ornament for the Essence:*

> As in the *Treatise on Pleasure,*[110] they enjoy coupling. Talking to each other about their pledges, they approach with a blissful mind. In short, since they would [otherwise] break their pledge, they attempt to remember their pledge well.

Thus he says not accepting the pleasure offered by a knowledge woman at a tantric feast is [also] the root downfall. This is directed toward certain [exceptional] people who have attained the capacity to rely on a knowledge woman as explained in the tantras, and for whom there are no other prohibitions. The *Saṃpuṭa Tantra* says this [not resorting to a knowledge woman] also breaks the pledge on other occasions [than feasts] as well. [474] Those without the capacity, and those who have gone forth to homelessness, should only resort to an imagined partner. The *Five Pledges:*[111]

> The external holy mudrā[112] embraces you. The students surround you, and they too embrace their knowledge woman. Those without the capacity do so with pure concentration.

Thus it makes an exception. The *Ornament of the Vajra Essence Tantra* probably means something similar when it says, "Those who have pledges do not play." Damtsigdorje and [Mañjuśrīkīrti's] *Commentary on the Root Downfalls* say this [downfall happens by] not resorting to the root and branch protection pledge. I do not see that as good. The *Ornament of the Guhyasamāja Tantra*, the *Clusters of Quintessential Instructions*, and the *Padminī Commentary on the Saṃvarodaya Tantra* designate this downfall just as it is here.

The Downfall in Yoga Tantra

The *object* is your "pledges," the vajra, bell, hand mudrā, and so forth. *The action that causes the downfall* is despising the vajra, bell, and hand mudrā, not resorting to them, and rejecting them. As for how you despise them, the second part of [Ānandagarbha's] *Long Śrīparamādya Commentary* says:

> It says, "without faith, ridiculing them." You break your pledge if, in a gathering of people, you despise the vajra and so forth [saying], "What purpose do they serve? Meditation alone is the main thing, not gesticulating with your hands and so on."

This, then, is how it occurs. The passage in which it is said to be a defeat was already cited above [385.1].

Question: Wouldn't this be the second downfall, not the thirteenth, because it would be willfully ignoring [a promise made to the Buddha]?

There is no flaw. There is [475] a big difference between the second root downfall, which is transgressing a rule by willfully ignoring it [with the thought], "There is nothing wrong with transgressing just this much," and [the thirteenth root downfall]. As in the *Long Śrīparamādya Commentary* cited earlier, this [thirteenth] is not resorting to and rejecting a pledge [with the thought], "Just by cultivating yoga practice, mentally the purpose of the vajra, bell, and so on is accomplished, so they are unnecessary." The former is not a root downfall relative to the lower [thirteenth] rule, but this [yoga tantra formulation of the thirteenth downfall] is a downfall relative to both [the second and the thirteenth vows].

The *Red* and *Black Yamāri Tantras* say, "Always resort to the pledges." Thus the downfall is not resorting to the pledges. A downfall like that explained above, then, is the thirteenth root downfall.

Fourteenth Root Downfall

> Fourteenth is despising women, whose essence is wisdom. [Mā 9ab]

This has two parts. The *object* is "women," either extraordinary ones such as Vajravārāhī who have taken the form of a woman, or any authentic woman. "Wisdom" means knowledge of great bliss. "Essence" can be taken in the sense of where something originates. It is said that [women] are the agent that produces that [knowledge of great bliss] in the yogi.

The action that causes the downfall is "despising" them. As for the way you despise them, relative to the former [extraordinary women], this refers to the expression of any fault whatsoever motivated by the desire to ascribe imperfection. Relative to the latter, motivated by the desire to ascribe imperfection, it is the voicing of criticism framed in terms that make it despising women in general. The *Root Downfall Commentary Amṛtacandra* and Lakṣmīṅkara say it is also necessary for the woman to understand [the insult], and in the latter case [476] it is probably so.

The *Kālacakra Tantra* and Dārikapa explain [this] relative to women in general in accord with this text, as do the *Clusters of Quintessential Instructions* and the *Padminī Commentary on the Saṃvarodaya Tantra*. As in the passage cited above [390.3] from Kāmadhenu's *[Commentary on the Cleansing All States of Woe Tantra]*, and in both the *Black Yamāri Tantra* commentaries, the root downfall is said to be despising Vajravārāhī and so forth, who has taken the form of a woman. This is common to both tantra sets. Here Damtsigdorje says the root downfall is despising Kurukulle and so on, and your own mudrā woman, and that it is a misdeed, as it were,[113] when it is other women. Certain other texts like the *Ornament of the Guhyasamāja Tantra* also say the root downfall is despising your own knowledge woman in particular. Nevertheless, our position is that although it is worse when it is your own mudrā, still, the root downfall is delimited as above. In the context of this argument Śāntipa says:

> Since wandering beings love women, among them are gods who have incarnated as women in order to pacify them. So you should not despise women.

Or he takes the position that you should not despise women because you do not know who is Vajravārāhī and so forth existing in the guise of a woman. It is clear, therefore, that he takes the general boundaries for the rule relative to just [undifferentiated] woman. So, although earlier in that [Śāntipa] commentary [on the *Black Yamāri Tantra*], he says that "woman" refers to Vajravārāhī and so on, he does not assert that it refers to them alone. Śāntipa goes on to cite the *Crown Jewel of the Guhyasamāja Tantra* as corroboration:

> When Tsangpa Punsumtsogpa Wangchug[114] ornamented his body, turned himself into a woman, and presented himself to the Victor Amitāyus, Śatakratu the Crested One said, "Sister, do not stand in front of the Tathāgata. [477] Do not be immodest."
>
> The Buddha said, "Speak when you have understanding, Devendra! You will get an unpleasant result from those [ill-considered words]. He is emanating as a woman in order to worship the Tathāgata and you should not call him a woman."
>
> After Śatakratu had begged his pardon, he said he really hoped he would not get that unpleasant result [that the Buddha had] mentioned. Then the bodhisattva Temochen[115] asked what the result would have been had Śatakratu not confessed.
>
> [The Buddha] said, "Had he not confessed, he would have been born as a woman eighty-four thousand times, so be careful of what you say!"

The *Red* and *Black Yamāri Tantras* and the *Ornament of the Vajra Essence Tantra* say that despising women is a misdeed, and the *Vajra Tent Tantra* also has "...disparaging the noble ladies..."

The root downfall of despising a genuine[116] woman does not apply in yoga tantra.

Here some say that if a woman despises a man it is a root downfall. There is neither an authoritative Indian scripture saying this, nor is it implied, since the root downfalls that I have explained earlier, as found in the tantras and authoritative Indian commentaries, are said to be downfalls for those with tantric vows in general, irrespective of whether they are male or female.

A downfall like that explained above, then, is the fourteenth root downfall.

Summary of the Root Downfalls

Now let us summarize these root downfalls. [478] The entire discussion about downfalls concerns rules for the purpose of stopping serious immoralities. There are three principle objects in relation to which misdeeds occur: those who teach us the Dharma, friends in our practice of the Dharma, and Dharma that has to be put into practice. The first downfall rule prevents immorality vis-à-vis the first. The second—friends—are of two sorts: perfect friends and those who have gone wrong. The third and twelfth downfall rules prevent us from doing wrong to the first, and the tenth downfall rule prevents us from making friends with the second. The Dharma is of two sorts: scriptural and practical. The second, sixth, and seventh downfall rules prevent us from treating a scripture as trivial, denying that it is the sacred word of the Buddha, and teaching it to those who should not be taught, respectively. Practical Dharma is threefold: the basis of the path, the actual path, and the aids to the path. The fourth rule prevents us from veering away from the living beings for whom we have produced bodhicitta, the basis of the path, and the fifth rule prevents us from giving up the actual bodhicitta. The nature of the path is twofold: the generation and the completion stages. The eighth downfall rule prevents abuse of the aggregates, which are the foundation for deity meditation. [Then there is] the completing stage. There are two [aspects to this]: right from the outset rejecting emptiness, and, even though you have realized it, neglecting to think about it. The ninth and the eleventh downfall rules prevent those two. The aids to the path are two: the pledges that underpin the path and [479] women who are friends on the path. The thirteenth and fourteenth downfall rules prevent not resorting to the first and despising the second, respectively. The *Commentary* said to be by Jowo [Atiśa] and Lakṣmīṅkara also gives a summary, but in a different way.[3]

5. How to Keep a Tantric Ordination

What to Do So You Are Not Degraded by a Downfall

Producing the Wish to Protect Yourself

PRODUCING THE WISH to protect yourself from becoming degraded by a downfall has two parts: thinking about the benefits of protecting, and the penalties of not protecting [the vows].

Thinking About the Benefits

> Mantric practitioners will definitely obtain siddhis if they avoid these. [Mā 9cd]

They "will obtain" what? All supreme and common "siddhis." Who? As the eighteenth section of [Śāntipa's] *Handful of Flowers Commentary on the Guhyasamāja Tantra* says:

> A mantra is your deity. Since they have those, they are mantric practitioners. They have firm pride in being such.

Thus they are practitioners with the meditative stabilization mantras of their deities. What do they do to obtain [the siddhis]? They will obtain them "if they" are not degraded by and "avoid these," the aforementioned root downfalls. It says "definitely" because there is no doubt that, having done that, they will obtain the siddhis. Both [eight-syllable] lines [of Mā 9cd] are in the *Ornament of the Vajra Essence Tantra.*

As for how they obtain the siddhis, Saraha in his *Commentary on the Difficult Points of the Buddhakapāla Tantra Called Jñānavatī* cites the *Treasury of Secrets* as saying:[117]

> If they have a perfectly bestowed consecration they will be consecrated life after life and obtain siddhi in seven lives even without meditation. If those who meditate and keep their pledges and vows do not obtain siddhi here because of the force of karma, [480] they obtain siddhi in another life. Those who break pledges not only will not obtain siddhis, but will find a human life hard to get.

Thus, as the passage he cites from the *Treasury of Secrets* says, even if they do not meditate with great effort in this life, in seven lifetimes they will obtain siddhi. It further says that those who meditate a little and have pure pledges and vows achieve that, but that those who break their pledges will not only not obtain siddhis, but will wander into states of woe and find a good rebirth only with difficulty. The *Five Pledges* says, "If they have not fallen, siddhi will be in sixteen lives." And Vibhūticandra [in his *Light Garland of the Three Codes*] also says,[118] "Even if they have not meditated, if they do not fall, siddhi will be in sixteen lives."

Thus they say that if they are not degraded by a root or branch downfall, or, if degraded, if they properly repair and protect their pledges and vows with purity, they will achieve the supreme siddhi within sixteen lives. As for the difference between seven or sixteen lives, as Vibhūticandra says, "even if they have not meditated..." Thus it depends on whether or not they are vigorous at meditation [not on whether they have or have not meditated at all], because the earlier [passage cited from the *Treasury of Secrets*] also says "...if those who meditate..." And it also says that if, "because of the force of karma," those who vigorously meditate on the path are incapable of supreme siddhi in this life, their pure pledges will give them siddhi within seven lives.

For those kind of pledges to be pure, mere purity in relation to the root downfalls is not enough. Purity relative to the branch pledges—the gross downfalls—must also be present, because the *Ornament of the Vajra Essence Tantra* says:

> Mantric practitioners who transgress these will definitely [481] meet up with Māra.[119] Sickness and suffering will increase, they will have no resting place, and they will go headlong to hell. Know that the penalty for gross downfalls is similar to that.

Thus it says that in those cases not only do they not obtain siddhis, but they also find a good rebirth only with difficulty.

Furthermore Jñānabodhi, citing many [scriptures], says [in his *Summary of the Beginner's Pledges*] that the assembly of victors, bodhisattvas, heroes, and heroines are pleased with them and protect them, so that their good qualities increase more and more, and Māra and so forth do not have a chance to cause harm. So think about these benefits and produce a great enthusiasm for guarding these pledges and vows.

Thinking About the Penalties

> Otherwise they break their pledges. Broken, they are possessed by Māra. Then they experience suffering and wander facing down in hell. [Mā 10]

"Otherwise they" do not avoid the downfalls as instructed. They "break" or transgress "their pledges," the rules, and, as māntrikas who have "broken" [the rules], face two penalties. The first penalty here is being "possessed by" or controlled by "Māra" and rogue spirits and so forth. "Then" all sorts of inauspicious things happen and "they experience" mental and physical "suffering." The penalty in a future life is to "wander" among living beings "in" the great "hells," "facing down," that is, in the intermediate state [482] they are upside down. As [Vasubandhu's] *Treasury of Knowledge* says, "...hell beings are upside down." The *Secret Ornamental Moon Spot Tantra:*

> Those who want mantra siddhis should try hard to guard the pledges. If the mantric practitioners do otherwise, the purposes of the mantras and so on are not accomplished. Even though they are requested by those with pledges, the gods do not appear to partake. Those confused individuals who transgress their pledged conduct experience great suffering in this world, and hells in the worlds beyond. Those disciples also suffer the depression that goes along with that. So, for disciples who do not keep their pledges intact, the purposes of mantra never ripen and they are never given the supreme bliss of the gods.

As for the meaning of "Even though requested by those with pledges, the gods," and so forth, Jñānabodhi [in his *Summary of the Beginner's Pledges*] cites the line, "They do not accept incense and flowers, and so forth, even if they are offered." Thus, even if those who transgress their pledges make offerings to buddhas and bodhisattvas, they do not partake. It also says that the ḍākinīs and so forth are cruel to those who break their pledges, and that the buddhas do not protect them. The thirty-eighth section of the *Little Saṃvara Tantra:*

> Brahmins whose pledges are destroyed and who behave badly are killed without a doubt. I do not protect those confused individuals who behave wickedly, led astray with a bad nature,[120] even if the ḍākinīs are feasting on them. They are like cattle among secret practitioners.

Even though this is talking about the careless recitation of the ḍākinīs' mantra, since it is similar [483] to breaking other pledges, Jñānabodhi cites it as scriptural basis for the penalties that pledge-breakers incur in general.

Hence you should keep the training of Vajradhara and make an effort to avoid the root downfalls explained above and the gross downfalls to be explained below, and not be like a *kunmanda* fruit[121] that is pretty on the outside but rotten inside—pretending to be a mantric practitioner externally, but with broken pledges and vows internally. Train as Abhayākara says in the fifth cluster of his *Clusters of Quintessential Instructions* immediately after speaking of the root and gross downfalls:

> Completely avoid them all by keeping the Vajrasattva training. Furthermore, here, on occasions after the time of actualizing the nondual,[122] trusting in the inconceivable simultaneously arisen practice and behaving just as you want, do not make just an outward show like the *kunmanda* fruit that is rotten inside.

The *Ritual Evocation of the One Who Owns the Entire Doctrine* also clearly says this. What it means is that at times afterward, when the state of suchness is not actualized, just from mere belief and trust in the inconceivable simultaneously arisen practice, you avoid doing what should not be done and you involve yourself [spontaneously and ethically] in anything and everything. Śāntipa also, in his *Jewel Lamp Commentary,* says:

> Therefore make an even greater effort to guard against these fourteen root downfalls, since that is the mantric practitioners' bedrock, as it were, their unyielding ground. If you see you have broken them, repair them as shall be explained. Otherwise, like a plantain tree with a [484] shriveled growth-bud, the remaining yoga practices will be incapable of bringing forth fruit.

Thus he says that the pledge to avoid the fourteen root downfalls is the main vital point, which mantric practitioners must vigorously guard. They should make sure they are not stained in the first place, and if they do break them, they should not just brush it off as inconsequential, but rather restore it in accord with the correct procedure. If they do not do so, the remaining meditation on the four yoga practices and so forth will not be capable of bringing forth their result, as with the example of the shriveled growth-bud of the plantain tree. When dealing with objections to this, he also says:

> How, then, do you interpret the statement that since even those who are extremely immoral will get siddhis if they have bodhicitta, they should practice without losing heart? That statement was made to elevate those who have fallen from the practice, or it is governed by [the consideration that it is] a first time [offense], or [it is said] out of a feeling of intense pity to take care of those who have given up all hope.

The master Jñānabodhi in his *Summary of the Beginner's Pledges* also says:[123]

> It is certain that the knowledge mantra must be kept, so if they do not correctly guard the vows and pledges they deceive the noble beings. Those cheats who turn their backs on siddhis are frauds, like a rotten tree. Those who do not keep the pledges, acting in various ways for themselves and others with a secret mantra that is just words, are like lepers dressed up in external finery and jewelry, but inside ravaged by disease. Never mind doing anything for [485] others, they cannot do anything even for their own benefit. Gods and humans look down on such people and rebuke them.

And [Mañjuśrīkīrti's] *Ornament for the Essence* says:

> Always consider the misdeed at the finish of even the tiniest gross downfall. Since mantric practitioners who have descended to mere words go to the Avīci hell and so forth, announce that you are a mantric practitioner and resort to the secret path, but do not ignore morality and give it up. Resplendent in white garments, having thrown all embarrassment to the winds, those lusting for immoral sex go to the hells of crying and wailing beings.

And:

> Having set forth in the Vajrayāna, settling down in attachment to things, willfully ignoring the path of dependent origination, and not applying yourself to wholesome activity, transgressing natural [morality] unconnected with time and need, doing the opposite of what is [normally] done in a region when unable to prevent others' lack of faith, and, unless you are pressured into it, or unless there is a great purpose, giving up your personal yoga and spiritual behavior are not in accord with the way. They at one and the same time break the orders of the Tathāgata and are downfalls, and hence damage the result. So make an effort and carry on in the three ways that do not break the pledges.

So you should think long on what is said in the sets of tantras and in their commentaries written by the wise—to wit, that the benefits of guarding [tantric vows] are [486] greater than those of guarding other vows, and the penalties for not guarding them are also greater. Become certain about the cause and effect of benefit and penalty, [that they are caused by guarding and not guarding the vows, respectively,] because when these two certainties are deep and real [in your mind], you will really guard your pledges and vows. When they are just mere words, you may guard your pledges and vows, but it will be nothing but mere talk.

Furthermore, you should not emulate those who do not see the whole range of the baskets of teachings and tantras, or who may see them, but do not check up with the explanatory tantras that excellently ascertain the many passages in the condensed tantras where you can go astray. They take the tantras literally, do not carefully consider [what they mean], and engage in vile behavior. Nowadays, as Śāntipa says, you must think long and hard before engaging in a practice. Those who are wise must do this.

However, those who do not see and listen to the Lord's sacred word in the precious sūtras and so forth—that is to say, the whole vast range of the sacred words of Buddha put into the baskets—and similarly those who do not see and listen to the action and yoga root tantras and their continuations, and the continuations of the continuations[124] that ascertain the meaning of the passages where you can go astray—take a few statements from some of the condensed tantras literally and speak in a totally inappropriate manner. They say that the Perfection literature and the action tantras and so on, which give instructions about karma and actions, are about the suffering path, a particular diet, and so forth, and about not behaving in whatever way you want; [487] and that this ocean-like highest yoga tantra is about how, as long as there is pleasure, no matter what you enjoy there is never any degeneration. They say that since pleasure depends upon enjoyment, women, liquor, meat, and so on are great offerings, are pure offerings, and are the speedy means of accomplishment.

The Lord, with the unhindered omniscience that views the three times, had a vision of this coming and said, "Seven hundred years after my nirvāṇa a wicked Māra will make a divisive explanation of my doctrines." In order to make just that known, he sealed his own doctrine with the three seals that are the sign of the doctrine and prohibited widespread propagation. He made a division between evil explanations and great disclosure,[125] setting forth his doctrine as though [gold] to be examined, washed, and scraped.[126] So in present times, those who have embarked on the doctrine would do well to examine it with an incisive intellect, and not, through a lack of investigation, get involved with other depravities.

Careless personal and interpersonal activities based on platitudes about emptiness—that anything is permitted for a yoga practitioner who realizes final reality—are also carefully excluded from what appears to be the way of secret mantra. The master Udbhaṭa Suraṅga [in his *Light on the Tantric Way*] speaks of this emphatically:[127]

> Our refuge has permitted those of us who are yoga practitioners of thatness whatever food and behavior and so forth we like. [488] And to make that clear, the *Secret Ornamental Moon Spot*

Tantra also says that there is nothing that yoga practitioners should not do.

In response to that he says:

> The Buddha has indeed said this to perfect yoga practitioners who realize emptiness and have compassion. In present times, no such persons are to be seen. You, who say that you should live here in this world like a complete buddha, doing whatever you want—why doesn't just one of your major marks of a buddha shine out? You who dislike our pledges say things that conflict with your being a receptacle for mantra doctrines. If you are practicing the sameness of substances in respect to food and drink, how amazing that you never practice by means of the paths of generosity and so forth. If you take yourself to be here like an illusion, why is your illusion hurt by hunger, thirst, and cold? The Friend of the World speaks to the mantric practitioners about what has a special accumulation. You do not have even a part of that, so how, without the cause, will the results ensue? [The statement] that enlightenment is attained with pleasure and that hardships are to be all abandoned is directed to the yoga practitioner working hard day and night at meditation, [not to you].

But I leave it at that because I fear this is getting too long.

What to Do So You Are Not Degraded: How to Guard Against Downfalls

> Therefore truly conquer pride, do not deceive yourself, and know [your vows]. [Mā 11ab]

Because it says that the benefits from guarding are very great and the penalties for not guarding [489] are very great as well, "therefore" māntrikas should strive to guard [their ordination]. How? Ārya Asaṅga [in his *Bodhisattva Levels*][128] systematizes the doors through which downfalls come into being as four. So the unsurpassed method for guarding the mind against a downfall is to block those four doors. Among these, not knowing the boundary relative to which a downfall does or does not occur is [1] unknowing that causes a downfall. So, to counteract that, "know" well the root and branch downfalls. Even if you know them, not respecting friends and so forth is [2] lack of respect that causes a downfall, so "truly conquer pride" and have respect. Even if you have respect, if you do not on occasion resort to conscientiousness, mindfulness, and vigilance, [3] a lack of conscience causes a downfall, so "do not deceive yourself," be guided by your conscience in all you do. And even though you know, respect and behave conscientiously, where afflicted emotions predominate, [4] the many obsessions cause a downfall, so, whichever of the other afflicted emotions instantiated by pride is greater, resort to its antidote as well, and focus on reducing its power. The *Vajra Tip Tantra:*

> If you break your pledges you will not get the fruit. If you break your pledge, here! this toast to hell [sealing your oath] will scald you. If you keep your pledge you will obtain siddhis. Drink up! Drink the vajra nectar. Swear an oath with this essence of the oath of Vajrasattva.

Thus it says that after pouring out the oath-water you should keep the pledges. And you must try to do so. You should protect them with the thought that even ordinary folk of the world [490] do not go back on an oath sworn in the presence of some minor opponent of the gods, so it goes without saying that it would be totally inappropriate if, having been sworn in as a practitioner of the Mahāyāna in general, and the Vajrayāna in particular, in the presence of the buddhas and their children, you do not at least commit to protect and restrain yourself in accord with the root pledges. So, the sort of effort you should devote to the pledges in general, and the root pledges in particular, is [huge]. As the *Saṃvarodaya Tantra* says, "If you want the supreme siddhi, continually guard your pledges, even giving up your life, even on pain of death." It also says that mantric practitioners who have gone forth to homelessness must try hard to protect not only their Mantra pledges, but their Prātimokṣa ordination as well. Dārikapa in his *Vajra Verses Explaining the Consecration* cites the following:

> Those who enter into this supreme great secret [maṇḍala] and declare themselves yoga practitioners, yet still engage in what should not be done, are thieves who corrupt the world.

After speaking at length, King Candrabhadra then said:

> Those not based in the well-spoken Vinaya, who do not guard it, who reject the Buddha's victory banner, and are defeated [by unwholesome behavior] and so forth do not know the excellence of drink, and swig down the intoxicating brew made with *sa-li-la,* thereby totally disgracing themselves.

Generally speaking, many mantric texts often say that prātimokṣa is needed even in the context of mantra. In the works of the Kālacakra cycle, in particular, the prātimokṣa is accorded importance in a number of ways—through making a hierarchy of [491] vajra holders in terms of a vajra holder who is also a monk and so forth, and through setting out the seating order when a master consecration is bestowed on a monk, a novice, or a layperson and so on.

How to Repair Broken Vows

> Mantric practitioners who want to benefit themselves, with composure, worshipping with whatever they have, should strive to take the bodhisattva ordination and so on starting with going for refuge to the Three [Jewels]. [Mā 11–12b]

If they guard [these vows] as explained above, but, through the force of a lack of conscience bring upon themselves one of the root downfalls of disparaging their master and so on, then, right away "with composure," single-pointedly, "worshipping" their guru as a gift prior to disclosure "with whatever they have" in line with their capacity, they should make a confession of those misdeeds in front of their guru. Then, "mantric practitioners who want to benefit themselves," or get immediate and future happiness, "should take the ordination" again. Which ordination? The "bodhisattva" ordination (the "and so on" brings in the Vajrasattva ordination) "starting with" or based on "going for refuge to the Three" Jewels. Furthermore, they should not think, "It would be good to do it, but if it is not done that is just the way it is." Rather, they should "strive" hard to take it. The *Vajrāvalī of Maṇḍala Rituals:*

> For misdeeds such as disparaging the guru and so on, having given what they can prior to disclosure, they should make a confession in the guru's presence [492] and retake the ordination as before.

Nagpopa says they should make a confession based on first telling their guru and vajra relatives assembled together in a tantric feast the misdeeds they have done.

Is a separate ritual for just proclaiming and taking the vows done by a guru sufficient, or does this have to be done in combination with consecration? [The *Vajrāvalī of Maṇḍala Rituals*] "...retake the ordination as before" means it has to be done exactly as before, when the ordination was first taken, in combination with a maṇḍala ritual. Even though this text just says take the ordination, and is not explicit about the need for consecration, it is definitely needed because the third chapter of the *Kālacakra Tantra* says, "Those who have incurred a downfall should again enter this maṇḍala in order to purify."

The seventeenth part of the *Black Yamāri Tantra* says, "If through lack of conscience they harm the guru [and] pledge, they should draw a maṇḍala and confess the misdeed to the tathāgatas."

Nagpopa takes "guru" and "pledge" separately, taking "pledge" to be the sacred words of the tathāgatas and saying that harming them is a downfall. Śāntipa, in the passage beginning, "Those who have disparaged their guru...," [says] if a root downfall occurs they should enter the maṇḍala and receive consecration. Thus he says, "If, to purify a root downfall that has occurred, they enter into a maṇḍala and obtain the sacred words, though they have fallen, it becomes a little purified." And [Ratnarakṣita in his] *Padminī Commentary* on the twenty-seventh chapter of the *Saṃvarodaya Tantra* says, [493] "If you fall from any of these, purify by taking the consecration again." Jñānabodhi [in his *Summary of the Beginner's Pledges*] also says the same.

Objection: Consecration is unnecessary because the vows are obtained during the ordination part of the maṇḍala ritual and returned to their former state.

Response: You have to purify the ordination through a consecration that combines both purification of wrongs and the taking of vows. It is not sufficient just to take the vows—you must also receive consecration as well. So [Mañjuśrīkīrti in his] *Commentary on the Root Downfalls,*

Lakṣmīṅkara, and the *Root Downfall Commentary Amṛtacandra* and so forth are completely wrong to say that the way to pick yourself up after every downfall, except the first root downfall, is independent of consecration. The author of the *Root Downfall Commentary Amṛtacandra,* therefore, seems to be masquerading under the name of Śāntipa. The *Commentary on Difficult Points to Do with Root Downfalls* says consecration is necessary.

Question: For this repair, is it definitely necessary to request a guru to bestow consecration, or can you do the self-consecration yourself? You can do the self-consecration if there are no fully qualified gurus present or, even if there are, if they are a long way off or if reaching them is dangerous. The *Vajrāvalī of Maṇḍala Rituals:*

> And if you break your pledge you should receive this same sort of consecration, taking [the ordination] just as the master explains it in the entering ritual. This is not [necessary], however, in other [circumstances] when the holy gurus are living in a distant region and you cannot get there because dangers make it hard to reach.

This and the passage cited earlier [400.3] from the *Ornament of Kosala* are outstanding, because otherwise you would [494] be extremely hard pressed to find a person holding [tantric] vows from whom you could take [the ordination].

You do this, thinking that you repair and restore [your vows] to their former state through consecration and by doing self-consecration. This does not happen, however, unless you have the thought of restraint deeply in your heart—unless you do not want to be degraded again by a downfall in the future. Dārikapa [in his *Vajra Verses*] says this clearly with an example:

> This, moreover, is for those committed not to do it again in the future, not for those without the intention to restrain in the future. [The latter] are like people who have been poisoned, who, after the doctor has poured them the antidote, go and eat the poison again.

Thus you restore [the ordination] to its former state if you get this [ordination] from generating [1] a feeling of regret for what you did in the past and [2] a strong thought to restrain from doing it in the future. Understand this.

Even though you do get the vows again by making a proper restoration, still, there is a world of difference between that and an ordination that has never, from the first, been punctured by a root downfall. For example, as it says in the *Bodhisattva Levels,* if those with bodhisattva ordination incur a root downfall, the ordination comes into being if they take it again, but they cannot attain the first pure concentration level in that life.[129] The *Vaidalya Compendium*[130] says that if someone with the misdeed of rejecting the Dharma mentioned there [in the *Bodhisattva Levels*] makes a confession three times a day for seven years, they will purify that wrong, but, whereas they would have quickly obtained the forbearance [stage],[131] now they will have to wait for ten eons. So as this says, if you properly repair a root downfall that, had it not been repaired, would have caused rebirth in hell and so forth, it is purified, [495] but the higher qualities of the path come about after a long delay. This is the same as my earlier explanation [445.2–5] of the first root downfall.

And they say that not just root downfalls, but any downfall is both an obstruction to the production of higher good qualities, and leads you down—so from the start try not to be degraded. And if you do end up with a root downfall, in particular, though you retake and receive the ordination, still the continuum is weakened, the qualities you had earlier degenerate easily, and those you did not have before are produced only with great difficulty. So as the *Saṃvarodaya Tantra* says [490.2], give even your life to [avoid] root downfalls. They say that saintly ones, seeing just how important this is, do not involve themselves in even a tiny downfall even at the cost of their lives. Unlike them, those for whom there is no difference between the purity [that arises from] confession and the purity [that arises when infractions] did not occur from the start, work just that much [at avoiding downfalls]. These [statements] are very important,[132] so I should cite the scriptural sources, but fearing prolixity I desist from setting them forth here.

You repair the downfalls by way of saying to another person just what your downfall is, spelling it out. Somebody with the ordination does this. And even in the case of a downfall that does not constitute a root downfall, since both Abhayākara and Nagpopa say that those with root downfalls make a prior confession to their guru, those who have discarded their ordination would do best to confess to their guru, or, if not, then to someone with tantric vows.

Although both master Nāgārjuna [in his *Vajra Vehicle Gross Downfalls*] and Aśvaghoṣa [in his *Gross Downfalls*] say you should make a confession if you incur a gross downfall, a separate clear and believable account of the correct way to make the confession is not to be found. The *Gross Downfalls Commentary* [496] attributed to Aśvaghoṣa says:[133]

> Among those, the repair. If they are rich, having thrown a heroes' party at a tantric feast, they confess by saying to them, in their presence, what they actually did. They request the retaking. Those objects [i.e., those who are being asked to hear the confession] should give water in the palm of the hand seven times, repeating the one hundred syllable [Vajrasattva mantra]. In the place of [the Sanskrit] *me* ["to me"] they should add the name [of the supplicant].

"In the place of *me* they should add the name" means that they should put the name of the one over there [i.e., the name of the supplicant who has broken the vow] wherever they find [the Sanskrit] *me* in *sa rva si ddhi me* [*prayaccha*] ["please give all siddhis to me"] and so forth. [Mañjuśrīkīrti's] *Ornament for the Essence* also says:

> The misdeed of a downfall and so on. Step-by-step you humble your mind, then when they have come to listen, take [the ordination] three times and confess transgressions three times.

Thus he says you repair it [by a ritual act said] to a person. This serves many purposes—it makes it easier to feel shame and embarrassment, it causes the boundaries of more and less important rules to be clearly marked, and it causes you to involve yourself in wrongdoing less in the future. So, though there are many ways to purify downfalls, this is a particularly important point.

Even though there are many tantric scriptures in which the ritual confession of misdeeds is directed to the buddhas and bodhisattvas, without delineating each particular wrong downfall, I have not seen a text that stands up to scrutiny as authentic in which [you are directed to] spell your downfalls out to a person in order to repair them. So, for a confession ritual, as in the practice of Sakyapa Jetsun [Dragpa Gyeltsen], use the bodhisattva ordination downfall-confession ritual [from the *Bodhisattva Levels*] with some minor alterations.[134]

It goes like this: first, make a prostration to the objects [of supplication, those] with tantric vows. Do this if they are senior to you. If they are younger, just behave respectfully. Then ask them to listen, "Please listen to my confession of the offenses [497] that I have committed, whatever they are." Then squat down below them, press your palms together and set out the matter.

> O master... (if it is your master, or "O knowledge holders..." or "O noble ones..." if they are friends) please pay heed to me. I, Akṣobhya, have incurred the offense of disparaging my master from among the four that have been described as defeats, constituting infractions of the Vajrayāna disciplinary code. I confess this to you, master (or knowledge holders), candidly and free of dissembling. Confessing and candid I am at ease; were I not candid and were I not to confess, I would not be at ease.

After saying this three times, the object [of supplication] inquires, "Do you see this as an offense?"

You reply, "I do see."

And [the object of supplication inquires], "From now on will you keep the vow?"

You reply, "I do assent to it in all humility, according to the doctrine and disciplinary code."

This exchange is done three times, and then the object [of supplication] says "Well done," and the one making the confession says, "Thank you." This is done one time.

[Ānandagarbha's] *Maṇḍala Ritual Called Sarvavajrodaya* has, in the context of the confession, "I, Vajra so-and-so..." so you should use your secret name.

Furthermore, [Mañjuśrīkīrti's] *Ornament for the Essence* says meditating on the two stages [of tantra], repeating [mantras], [offering] ritual cakes and maṇḍalas, confessing in front of receptacles,[135] saving the lives of living creatures, reading sacred words, making clay statuettes stamped with a sacred image,[136] imagining your wrongs as sesame seeds and burning them, summoning and [498] emptying the states of woe, and reciting the *Three Heaps Sūtra* and so on purify immorality and downfalls. And it says, "If you are always without any conscience, even your tiny, little misdeeds will injure your body, speech, and mind, like a nip from the fang of a snake." Thus it says that if you have no conscience, even minor immorality intensifies, like poison from a bite. It also explains how to prevent intensification after a downfall has occurred:

> Clearly visualize Vajrasattva, the single form of all buddhas, with a vajra and bell, radiantly adorned and seated on a white lotus in the center of a moon. Recite the one-hundred-syllable [mantra] twenty times for each [of body, speech, mind, and the unity of those three]. The holy practitioners say that because of the blessing, downfalls do not increase. So do this in the period between meditation sessions. If you repeat it one hundred thousand times, [the downfall] is essentially purified.

They say that Amoghasiddhi also has the name Samayavajra and that he is a deity especially for the purification of broken pledges. The *Samāntabhadra Ritual Evocation* written by [Buddha]jñāna-pāda, the son of Mañjuśrī, and its offshoots have the instructions for purifying disparagement of your guru and so on through this door [of Samayavajra]. You should also do this between meditation sessions, but again, fearing prolixity, I refrain from writing about it here.

Conclusion

> The *Vajrayāna Root Downfalls* composed by the master Bha-bi-lha is complete. [Mā 12cd]

This root text appears to simply teach the names of the root downfalls gathered from tantric literature. The [499] *Clusters of Quintessential Instructions,* the *Padminī Commentary on the Saṃvarodaya Tantra,* and the *Ritual Evocation of the One Who Owns the Entire Doctrine* give them similar names. There does not seem to be an authoritative commentary on this text. In those that do exist there are many disagreements. There do not seem to be any commentaries for either the *Red Yamāri Tantra* or the *Ornament of the Vajra Essence Tantra,* and the two *Vajra Tent Tantra* commentaries[137] and Śrīdhara's and Kumāracandra's two commentaries on the *Black Yamāri Tantra* have no explanation of the root downfalls, so it is extremely difficult to precisely demarcate what you transgress, or do not transgress, to incur a root downfall. Nevertheless, I have based all except the explanation of the eleventh root downfall on Śāntipa's *Jewel Lamp Commentary on the Black Yamāri Tantra* and I have generally cited the explanation in Nagpopa's *Lamp to View the Path Commentary on the Black Yamāri Tantra* as well. Occasionally I have borrowed passages from the better parts of the commentaries [on the root downfalls] that borrow the voices of Mañjuśrīkīrti, Aśvaghoṣa, Śāntipa, Jowo [Atiśa], and Nyingpo,[138] as well as the commentary by Lakṣmīṅkara. I have also brought in other tantric texts.

6. Gross Downfalls, and the Downfalls in the Kālacakra System

SECOND, the explanation of the gross downfalls *(sthūlāpatti)* has two parts: the meaning of the title [of the text used as a basis for the explanation] and the meaning of the text. First, it is called *Vajrayāna Gross Downfalls*. I explained "vajra" and "downfall" earlier. One of a number of [Tibetan] translations for *sthūla* is *chen po* ("large"). Relative to the Vajrayāna vows, it is all the remaining misdeeds, other than the class that constitutes downfalls.

The Meaning of the Text

The meaning of the text has three parts: introductory activities, the composition of the explanation itself, and [500] the conclusion.

Introduction

First:

> Having bowed down with complete respect to the lotus feet of my guru, I shall explain the eight gross downfalls spoken of in the tantras. [Sā 1]

This, too, you can understand from my earlier explanation [440.3–6]. In general, there are infinite gross downfalls. This does not teach them all. Rather it teaches by systematizing the gross downfall class of infractions in terms of eight main entrances.

The Explanation of the Gross Downfalls

First Gross Downfall

Second, the composition of the explanation itself has eight parts. About the first gross [downfall] it says,

> Violently appropriating a wisdom woman *(prajñā)*... [Sā 2a]

This is to be construed with, "These are the eight gross downfalls," which comes later.[139] "Prajñā" means a woman. "Appropriate" means to resort to her as a knowledge woman [i.e., partner]. "Violently" means to resort to her as a knowledge woman just through your own power, without thoroughly training her. To thoroughly train is to ripen the mindstream with consecration, make an array of the pledges and vows, and teach mantra and tantra well. The master Aśvaghoṣa says [in his *Gross Downfalls*], "Enjoying a knowledge woman without pledges violently, and also abusing her, is said to be the first downfall of this yoga."

The *Commentary* to this says there are three gross [downfalls] here—when a woman without pledges is unripened by consecration, or if consecrated, is sick, keeping particular vows to do with marriage or the propitiation of a particular deity and so forth,[140] or timid, it is a gross [downfall] to resort to and pressure her while she does not assent, to abuse her from the standpoint of limbs and so on, and to ridicule her so that she becomes upset. The *Ornament of the Vajra Essence Tantra* says [501] resorting to a knowledge woman without pledges is a gross [downfall]. The earlier text [Sā] does not make a separate mention of the absence of pledges, so construe the meaning of violence as before, and also construe it more generally as does the later explanation.

Second Gross Downfall

> Violently appropriating her nectar... [Sā 2b]

Violently appropriating the nectar of that knowledge woman is a gross [downfall]. Here Aśvaghoṣa says, "...also resorting to nectar in just those stages not spoken of in the tantras." The *Commentary* to this says that:

> Enjoying without divine pride, without having been blessed, in front of those without faith, and other than at special times is a downfall. It is resorting in stages[141] prohibited by the tantras.

Third Gross Downfall

> Not keeping secrets from those who are not vessels... [Sā 2c]

Abhayākara and Ratnakīrti say "not keeping secrets" is not concealing. If you do not keep secret, do not conceal, if you reveal secret materials such as pictures of the deity's form, the sacred texts, the six ornaments and so forth, and if you reveal the mudrā's clasp to "those who are not vessels," those without consecration, or to those who, if they are consecrated, do not have faith, it is a gross [downfall]. The third part of the ninth section of the *Saṃpuṭa Tantra* says:

> If just the text and pictures of the body are seen by those without good fortune, you will get no siddhis in this life, and not encounter them in the world beyond.

The [Guhyasamāja] explanation tantra *Vajramālā* says "...with great effort..." Thus you get siddhis only after a very long time if you reveal pictures of the body to non-vessels and so on. Certain Tibetans [502] say that since you will not be able to practice [in rituals conducted before large gatherings of people] without appearing widely with your vajra and bell, hold your private pledge vajra and bell, [i.e., the consecrated ones you use in private practice] without showing them [and keep another set for use on those occasions]. This rule seems to be a good one. The first part of the *Compendium of Principles* says, "Do not show any mudrā at all to anyone else who does not understand mudrās." Its *Illumination* provides the gloss, "Do not even let them peek." That is also the branch downfall that some[142] mean when they talk about "not revealing the mudrā to those not skilled in mudrā."

Fourth Gross Downfall

> Quarreling in the assembly... [Sā 2d]

If you quarrel in a tantric feast or at all-male or all-female ritual parties it is a gross [downfall]. The *Commentary on the Gross [Downfalls]* says, "If you have entered, you have to have divine pride, love for living beings, and the attention of a ritual priest collecting the equipment [for enlightenment], so if you quarrel with each other, or physically give so much as a slap, it is a gross [downfall]." Two commentaries on the *Five Stages*[143] say that this is a defeat. That is not the meaning.

[Mañjuśrīkīrti's] *Ornament for the Essence:*

> On no account engage in idle chatter intent on making [worldly] relationships, because if you do the result you get is hell and so forth. If you talk behind a person's back during worship you will become a denizen of the Roaring hell, if you are obsessed with need you will definitely become a *preta,*[144] and if you lose your concentration you will descend to the animal [realm].

Thus it also mentions [503] the penalties for disparaging others and so on during a tantric feast.

Fifth Gross Downfall

> Teaching a different doctrine to the faithful... [Sā 3a]

The *Commentary* says when "the faithful," or those who are suitable vessels, ask about the Dharma, it is "teaching a different doctrine." For example, teaching about covering level marks when asked about ultimate marks. Aśvaghoṣa also says, "If you teach other than the true nature of dharmas to the faithful when they ask about the Dharma, the Jina has said that that is the fifth downfall described as gross."

Sixth Gross Downfall

> Living among listeners for a week... [Sā 3b]

"Living among" followers of the "Listener" Vehicle who are repulsed by secret mantra "for a week" (up to six days is permitted) is a gross [downfall]. They say there is no misdeed if you are in mortal danger and so on, or if you do it to obey government orders.

Seventh Gross Downfall

> Being deceitfully pretentious about yoga practice... [Sā 3c]

[Aśvaghoṣa's] *Commentary* says pretensions to understanding suchness and teaching it based on just doing the ritual evocation of the deity is a gross [downfall]. Abhayākara says this is pretensions about a yoga practice when you do not know the yoga practice. They both mean the same thing. This is the sort of gross [downfall] we are prone to these days.

Eighth Gross Downfall

> Teaching to the faithless... [Sā 3d]

This is the gross [downfall of] "teaching" mantra secrets [1] to those never matured by consecration "who" have no "faith" in mantra, and [2] to those consecrated or matured, but who have no faith in mantra and believe in the outer [non-Buddhist tantra]. [504] Aśvaghoṣa says, "Revealing secret doctrines to living beings who are not vessels, and to those who believe in the outer..."

I have already explained the misdeed of disclosing mantra secrets to those not matured by consecration in the root downfall section [456.6–460.4].

Concluding Remarks

> These are the eight[145] gross downfalls. [Sā 4a]

I have already explained this [500.3].

> Know the sequences of the gross [and] root downfalls. Make a ritual confession if you degenerate. [Sā 4b–d]

What it means is "know the root downfalls" and "gross" [downfalls], and "if" your continuum "degenerates" because of them, "make a confession" in line with the "ritual." Aśvaghoṣa says, "If [a downfall] happens and they make a confession in line with ritual, they do not go to hell."

Third, the conclusion.

> The *Vajrayāna Gross Downfalls* composed from the mouth of the master Nāgārjuna is complete. [Sā 5]

The *Clusters of Quintessential Instructions,* the *Ritual Evocation of the One Who Owns the Entire Doctrine,* and the *Padminī Commentary on the Saṃvarodaya Tantra* also give the eight gross downfalls as they are explained here. Aśvaghoṣa's text on gross downfalls is not at variance. The twelfth part of the *Ornament of the Vajra Essence Tantra* says:

> Resorting to a knowledge woman without pledges, quarreling in a tantric feast, revealing secret doctrines and teaching differently to the faithful, staying with listeners for a long time, and teaching secrets to non-vessels are gross immoralities. They end the mantric practitioners' ordination, and when it has ended they accomplish nothing. So read them out loud three times every day.

Thus it says that [505] those with gross downfalls, like those with root downfalls, are given no siddhis when they practice and, as cited earlier [504.3], are hurled into hell. Even though it teaches just six gross downfalls here, [all eight are included]. The first two mentioned above are subsumed in the first, because violently appropriating a wisdom woman is the downfall of using an unqualified partner, and violently appropriating her bodhicitta is the downfall of resorting to a qualified partner, but not in the way that the tantras say. [The third and the seventh are subsumed in the third] because revealing secret doctrines has a twofold division—revealing pictures of the [deity's] form and mudrās, and teaching by those with pretensions of being a practitioner. You should know the gross downfalls are also mostly the same in yoga tantra.

Furthermore, Lakṣmīṅkara gives a commentary on the following:

> Enjoying a knowledge woman without pledges, quarreling in a tantric feast, teaching the holy Dharma differently to living beings with faith, passing more than seven days among those who are conceited about being listeners, disclosing secrets to the unfortunate who have not been properly prepared, revealing

> body mudras to those unskilled in mudrās, engaging in maṇḍala work without having fully done the long retreats[146] and so on, and transgressing rules of the two ordinations when there is no need...

Apart from occasionally different phrasing, this is found in the *Compendium of All the Pledges* as well. I do not know which tantra it is taken from. Lakṣmīṅkara says [you disclose secrets to those] "who have not been properly prepared" [506] if, without special need, you teach the three things connected with consecration to those who, having broken the pledges they got before, no longer have them, and they understand. "[Engaging in maṇḍala work] without having properly done the long retreats and so on" is setting out to bestow consecration on others without having properly done a long retreat, [determined either in terms of a specific] number [of mantras you recite, a specific] length of time [you will spend], or [ending only when] signs [of success appear, such as] a fire offering and deity yoga, and so forth. He teaches that "transgressing rules of two ordinations when there is no need" is, for instance, when a vajraholder who is a fully ordained monk commits a tantric gross [downfall] and two minor transgressions of the other [Vinaya] ordination from doing [an unnecessary] *homa* rite, because of being mindful of the feeling of the fire and making the grain unusable, [which are both Vinaya transgressions]. I have explained the rest before.

[Mañjuśrīkīrti's] *Commentary on the Root Downfalls* gives an explanation of eight, fifteen, and seven branch misdeeds that is somewhat different from these. The latter two [lists of branch misdeeds] are also found in the *Compendium of All the Pledge Rituals.* But I will not write about them here because the latter [text] seems to say that all fifteen are root downfalls spoken of in the *Kālacakra Tantra,* whereas, [as branch downfalls] they do not have the import of root downfalls. Also [that text] does not appear to be a reliable scripture, and I have not seen [this cited] in any other learned person's work. Understand, therefore, that Jowo [Atiśa] did not compose the *Compendium of All the Pledge Rituals.*

These, then, are the most important of the pledges. The tantras give the details of an infinite number of them. As for the food pledge mentioned in the context of highest yoga tantra, namely that they should resort to the five meats and nectars, new practitioners should, if they can, heed statements about making pills and resorting to them [507] each day. If they cannot, they can cause what they eat and drink to become such by means of mere concentration, and enjoy them. The *Five Pledges* says, "If you cannot obtain any, or are worried that those [in the vicinity] are not vessels [suitable to witness it], concentrate on imagining the five meats and nectars."

You should keep your pledges to retain a vajra, bell, and rosary, and so on at hand in the same way. [Mañjuśrīkīrti's] *Ornament for the Essence* says, "Having imagined secret materials, never be separated from the pill pledge, and from your implements such as vajra, rosary, and so forth." And the *Vajra Tent Tantra* also says, "pick out your vajra and bell," and so on.

The Kālacakra Tantra

Third is ascertaining the explanation of downfalls in the *Kālacakra Tantra*. Since most of the presentation in the *Kālacakra Tantra* differs in many ways from the standard explanation given in other tantras, I will teach it separately. This has two parts: how they take vows and actual downfalls that break them.

How Vows Are Taken

The Consecration chapter [of the *Kālacakra Tantra*]:

> In the desire Vajra [family] venerate the vajra, bell, mudrā, and guru; in the Jewel [family] give gifts; in the Wheel [family] guard the supreme victory pledge; in the Sword [family] offer worship; in the Lotus family brightly protect restraints; in the family of the Producer of Victory produce the bodhicitta essence[147] to liberate all beings.

With this, during the fundamental stage [of consecration], they take the vows. [508] In this it says that those "in the Vajra" family, take four [pledges], "vajra, bell, mudrā, and guru." Those "in the Jewel" family "give" ten "gifts," and, "the ten gifts are held to be jewels, iron, copper, cows, horses, elephants, girls, mines, a desirable wife, and your own flesh."

Those "in the Wheel" family guard the five meats and five nectars, the aggregates, and the collection of senses. Those in the Lotus family protect the restraint of chaste non-emission. Those "in the Sword" family "offer worship" to the Three Jewels; and those in "the Producer of Victory" single-spoke vajra "family" should "produce" the mahāmudrā siddhi that is empty and compassionate. Thus, some earlier [pledges] have differences from [the pledges in] other [tantras, even though the names for them are similar], and this latter [pledge] is not in other [tantras]. Still, since they get the ordination just by promising to protect the Akṣobhya family pledges and so on, the ordination comes into being in a similar way.

Some say that since the *Stainless Light Commentary* says, "...a prayer to promise to do those," this is not the taking ordination [section of the Consecration chapter], and the tantric vows come into being when all the consecrations are complete. They are wrong, because if this is not the ordination ritual, then the *Kālacakra Tantra* system has no ritual for taking the five family ordination.

[Objection]: The ritual for taking ordination is when [the master] gives the twenty-five rules specific to [Kālacakra practice]. That is wrong, because the master is simply teaching them to "stop the four—murder and so on, and beer and so on," not doing a ritual for students to take [ordination], and because [509] those [passages] are not concerned with the way to take unshared tantric vows. [The *Stainless Light Commentary*] says "prayer," [which might lead some to mistakenly think he is talking about a stage prior to ordination proper], to say that they take them having prayed to protect them. If just that [word "prayer"] excluded taking ordination, then every ordination ritual in which they take vows with the thought that they want to do what they have been told would no longer be a ritual for taking vows. And [they are wrong to say that tantric vows come into being merely when all the consecrations are complete, without ordination], because the *Kālacakra Tantra* says, "The root downfalls of those with good qualities who have the seven consecrations are purified." Thus it says that those who have obtained just the seven consecrations of water and so on get root downfalls, and in the absence of an ordination, root downfalls could not happen.

As for the vows held in common, since [the *Tantra*] instructs them to produce bodhicitta and to resort to the path of the ten perfections, they have to take [bodhisattva ordination] as well. The *Vajrāvalī of Maṇḍala Rituals* also does not have a separate explanation of the way those who enter into the Kālacakra maṇḍala take vows, so [Abhayākara] accepts that they take them in the general, five-family ordination style of taking found in other tantras, and he accepts that the ordination ritual is also similar in content. Nevertheless, [he says Kālacakra] differs from other [tantras] in the following respects: it includes two different ways of bestowing higher consecrations, there are specific directions—the north and so forth—for bestowing the water consecration and so on, and just bestowing the seven consecrations gives the five family ordination. These different features make it different from the other [tantras].

Actual Downfalls That Break Vows

The Consecration chapter:

> The children's moon [i.e., bodhicitta] root downfall [510] arises from upsetting the glorious guru's mind; the other arises from disobeying orders, and definitely a third arises from anger at relatives. The fourth arises from giving up love; the arrow arises from weakening bodhicitta. The sixth arises from disparaging a system of tenets. Mountains arise from giving secrets to immature people and *nāgas*[148] arise from hurting the aggregates. Again, the ninth arises from no faith in the pure Dharma, the directions, and *krodhas*[149] arise from a false show of affection, and conceptuality when given bliss free from words, and so forth. The sun arises from criticizing pure beings and another arises from[150] giving up the pledges they have. And Manu definitely arises from despising all women. Those who are in the Vajrayāna incur these.

"Those who are in the Vajrayāna" teaches the bases [i.e., people] in which the root downfalls are produced—those on whom consecration has been bestowed and who have taken ordination. "The moon" is a name for one, hence the first downfall is repulsing a "guru's mind." Here "guru" means your vajra master. Furthermore, [the *Tantra*] says that since good people would not selfishly cause upset, this is to do with altruism, and the root downfall happens when students have set out to do a wrong that disturbs the guru's mind. Dārikapa [in his *Vajra Verses*] says it is a root downfall when six conditions are met: [1] they know the guru is good, [2] they know [their action] is disagreeable, [3] there is a physical or verbal act motivated by an afflictive emotion, [4] [the action] is not altruistic, [5] their selfish intention dominates, and [6] they have no intention of correcting themselves. [511]

"The other" is the second downfall. It is "disobeying" that good guru's "orders," being told but not listening. [The *Tantra*] just says doing the ten non-wholesome acts hidden away from the guru. Dārikapa says it includes the above six, and that they have to set out to do a wrong, having broken Dharma orders that were directed specifically at them. Thus the former occurs when the guru has not given them orders [to desist], they set out to do some wrong, they know the guru is displeased out of concern for the student, but they think nothing of it and set out to do the wrong [regardless]. Here the guru has no displeasure, but contravening their guru's orders, having thought nothing of them, they have set out to do a wrong. The length of time they have no thought to make amends is not clear, but you should take it [to mean] from the start of the act up to right after it is completed.

"Anger at relatives." Although the *Stainless Light Commentary* says nothing except "anger at vajra relatives in training," [Puṇḍarīka's] *In Service to the Ultimate* says, "Third is speaking out of anger to a relative," so it seems to be like the earlier [449.5ff] explanations [of the third root downfall]. Dārikapa explains that there are the six prerequisites mentioned earlier and a seventh, being a vajra relative. [So the third] is breaking orders to do with relatives out of anger. Hence the first two [of Dārikapa's six prerequisites] change to "they know they are good [vajra] friends and they break their orders." Apart from saying they are relatives brought together by a single guru, Dārikapa does not explain how they are brought together.

[The *Tantra*] says that [512] "giving up love" is minor when, like a picture drawn in water, you are without it for a moment but it comes right back. It is middling when it is like a picture drawn in sand that is scattered and ruined by wind. It is great when it is like a clod of earth dissolved by summer floods, and very great when it becomes like separated rocks that will not combine again. The downfall occurs when giving up love is like that [very great]. It does not say how long it lasts, but Dārikapa says they do not produce a feeling of love for at least twenty-four hours.

The "bodhicitta" is seminal fluid, that is, it says the root downfall is the desire to get enlightened by the first two non-suchness blisses. It seems that motivated by that intention, they "weaken" their seed. Dārikapa says four conditions have to be met for a root downfall: [1] they know the nature of immutable bliss, [2] they intend to experience mere mutable bliss, [3] they hold that to be excellent, and [4] it is not altruistic, or for pills and so on.

"The sixth." The *Stainless Light Commentary* says, "The 'system of tenets' is the Perfection of Wisdom and, in tantra, the Tattvatā chapter. 'The sixth' is any disparagement of those." As for how you disparage, Dārikapa says, "The 'system of tenets' is the Perfection Vehicle. Taking that and tantra to be different is a root downfall." Thus, as he explains, it is disparaging by taking the suchness of the two—the Perfection of Wisdom and the Mantra Vehicles—to be worse and better, respectively. He further says that if all five: [1] Pāramitāyāna inseparable from Mantrayāna, [2] getting angry [513] and saying something disparaging, [3] having no altruism, [4] taking [the view] to be excellent, and [5] feeling no regret are complete, it is a root downfall, and that disparaging other vehicles does not constitute a root downfall, but steals away ordinary siddhis. This is simply disparaging, not forsaking [the Perfection of Wisdom by denying that it is] the sacred words of a buddha.

"The mountains" are the seventh. The statement that "immature people" are those on the listener's path gives an instance of those without faith in mantra. As for "secrets" voiced publicly, [the *Tantra*] says, "The masters have a downfall from giving great bliss." Thus this is when they publicize the secret of indivisible bliss and emptiness. In reference to publicizing secrets, Dārikapa says that when three things—[1] [the presence of] a non-believer, [2] [the lack of someone] to be trained, and [3] teaching the secret of great bliss—are complete, it is the root downfall, and that teaching secrets other than the secret of great bliss are downfalls that reduce ordinary siddhis. He is unclear as to whether those [who are told] have or have not been consecrated. It appears that they should not have been consecrated, however, because [Puṇḍarīka's] *In Service to the Ultimate* is making a general statement when it says, "Mountains are from being open with non-māntrikas." "Non-māntrikas" are those who have not been consecrated. "Being open" is making a secret not a secret. And the *Stainless Light Commentary* seems to be giving the primary instance when it says "...the secret which is great bliss."

The "serpent spirits" are the eighth downfall of hurting the aggregates. [The *Tantra*] says this [514] is fasting[151] and so on, and physical mutilation and so on. It is willfully "hurting" or causing suffering to your body by heat and cold, cutting off food and drink, and severing limbs. Dārikapa says that if you commit suicide, it is a root downfall the moment you decide to do it, and that when three things are complete it is a root downfall. These are [1] knowing that the aggregates are the jinas, goddesses, and bodhisattvas, [2] knowing that from torturing them bliss has declined, and [3] there is no need to tame others. Some say, "If yoga practitioners meditating on themselves as deities fast and cut off food and drink it is a root downfall." This is an extremely ill-considered statement, because [1] in action and performance tantras both deity yoga meditation and fasting are mentioned, [2] it is said that even masters who have finished the meditation and recitations of the Vajradhātu [maṇḍala of the *Compendium of Principles*], for instance, and can set out the vase and so on in space still do the fasting practice, and [3] because [Ānandagarbha's] *Maṇḍala Ritual Called Sarvavajrodaya,* having explained as above the qualities of a master who has already done the long retreats and so on says, "On the day they enter the maṇḍala, both master and disciples should fast."

Hence, since the fast that leads to the eighth downfall has been set forth as willfully hurting your body with the express intention of causing torment to your aggregates, it has the same name as "fasting," but does not have the same meaning.

"The pure Dharma" is emptiness. As Dārikapa explains, to have "no faith" in it is to reject the profound emptiness that has eliminated all grasping. He also says that when two things—[1] not for the purpose of taming others and [2] rejection of emptiness and acceptance of the adventitious—are complete, it is a downfall.

The "directions" are the tenth. It is "a false show of affection." This is said to be saying one thing while harboring something else in your heart. *In Service to the Ultimate* also says, "Directions are harboring venomous love," by which it seems to mean saying something affectionate while feeling venomous inside. Still, Dārikapa says that this means making a show of guarding the pledges in order to obtain profit and praise, all the while furtively doing unwholesome acts.

The *Stainless Light Commentary* says, "The 'krodhas,' that is, the eleventh, is any 'conceptualization when given the bliss free from words,' or the suchness of the tathāgatas." It only says that. Dārikapa, explaining this, says:

> It is a root downfall if they have "conceptualization," in other words, do not accept because of reservations or doubts, "when

> given" the suchness essence of the body, speech, and mind of all tathāgatas. In the mantra system, this [suchness essence] is the bodhicitta moon's incomparable, unchanging bliss.

He also says that when three aspects are complete [the downfall occurs]. The three are: [1] it is not changeable bliss, [2] it is unchangeable bliss beyond examples, and [3] it is not for the purpose of training others. Of these, the first seems unnecessary. *In Service to the Ultimate* says, "Indra[152] 'krodhas are conceptualization' about pure dharmas."

The "sun," the twelfth, [arises] "from criticizing pure beings," or yoga practitioners. [The *Tantra* and *Commentary*] say nothing beyond that. Dārikapa says that when [the following] three things are complete: [516] [1] [the presence of] a yoga practitioner with a yogic disposition, [2] a statement made out of envy, and [3] [made] not for the purpose of training others, it is the root downfall. *In Service to the Ultimate* says, "The sun is from repulsing pure beings," so you have to criticize them directly and repulse their minds.[153]

The thirteenth [arises] "from giving up the pledges they have" in a tantric feast. This is what the *Stainless Light Commentary* says. Dārikapa says this means that when [1] the time [for keeping] the pledge to do with, for instance, food during tantric and hero feasts is at hand, [2] they are not saving another's face, and [3] it is not for the purpose of training others, if, when the time has come, they do not accept food, drink, and *me-thu-na* with a woman, it is a root downfall. "Methuna"[154] means merging with a knowledge woman. This is based on yoga practitioners who have attained the capacity for such acts.

"Manu," the fourteenth, arises from despising women. "Definitely" without any doubt, there is a downfall "from despising all women." The object that is despised may be a single individual, but the despising words are framed in terms of women in general. Since Dārikapa mentions that this is not for the purpose of training others, they have to say it as a criticism and they have to understand it as well.

The *Stainless Light Commentary* says, "The gross downfalls are many. For them, the punishments are much smaller."

I have explained these before [500–506].

Thus there are similarities between these root downfalls and the standard ones given in the other tantras and explained earlier, but you cannot say the first two root downfalls, the fifth (giving up prayer bodhicitta) and the sixth (rejecting the doctrine), have the same meaning. [517] So how should those with highest yoga tantra vows treat them? Kālacakra and other highest yoga tantras have many differences in the way they bestow consecrations and set forth maṇḍalas. So, just as, for example, the followers of Cakrasaṃvara pledge to take and eat food with the left hand, similarly, perhaps, those who enter the maṇḍala and have been consecrated with the ritual explained in the Kālacakra, and those consecrated in other ways, each have their own orders to follow.

Alternatively, Śāntideva puts together just the eight defeats explained in the *Bodhisattva Levels* with many defeats different from those, explained in the *Ākāśagarbha Sūtra,* and talks of general root downfalls for an ordained bodhisattva. Similarly, [here in tantra,] you could formulate basic root downfalls for those with ordination, within taking [downfalls] like these [explained above in the standard and Kālacakra systems] as each implying the other. The intelligent should look into what is tenable. I have based myself on one line of explanation[155] while rejecting others as if they were incorrect, not explaining them as a single topic. This is like the difference between trainees when [a subject is] set forth relative to those to be trained. [The subject is the same, but what the listeners hear differs.] Hence, I have not found valid reasons to specify with certainty that this is set down as a rule and this is not set down as a rule. Nevertheless, it seems that even though you do not find displeasing the guru [in the list of downfalls], you have to assert that if followers of the Kālacakra displease a guru in the way explained earlier in the context of the standard norm for tantra, it is a root downfall, and, in particular, it seems that you have to set forth giving up prayer bodhicitta and forsaking the good Dharma [518] as root downfalls [in Kālacakra as well]. So, although I have not found any valid reasons, I do believe it is correct to make a composite of the practices and, regardless of what system it is a root downfall in, to be confident in the thought to avoid being degraded by them.

The explanation of the penalties for breaking pledges and how they are restored in the Kālacakra is in the Consecration chapter, "If they incur root downfalls through hypocritical consecration, they go to hell. These are suffering."

The *Stainless Light Commentary:*

> "If they incur root downfalls" that I will be explaining "through hypocritical consecration," or "through consecration that has

> set them into the ten non-virtues, all "these," their consecration and so on, become "suffering" in "hell" because, definitely, they have been wrongly consecrated.

The *Stainless Light Commentary* also says:

> "Those who have incurred a root downfall should, in order to purify it, again enter into this maṇḍala." This means that here, when those who have taken the seven consecrations, or have taken the vase and secret consecrations, incur a root downfall, in order to purify it, having drawn this maṇḍala they should again enter into the maṇḍala, and so on so that they will not [incur the downfall] again. Then, having received permission, again "in the feast assembly," or in the midst of the family, "what was a high name before becomes small, becomes youthful," [i.e., with] the certainty of a tathāgata, students should have no doubt about their vow not to do it again.

Thus it says that to repair it they have to do [the restoration] specifically [519] so that they will not do that [deed that constitutes the downfall] again. This is very important.

How could it say that "consecration and so on become" causes of "suffering in hell"? The *Sūtra About What Is Important for Bhikṣus* says, "For some morality is happiness and for some morality is suffering. Being moral is happiness and fake morality is suffering." This intends to say that if you guard an ordination after committing yourself to it, you are happy, but if you do not guard it, you create suffering. And as [the *Vajra Tip Tantra,* cited 489.5] said, "If you break your pledge, here! this toast to hell..." Thus understand that [the water for consecration] is both hell-water and nectar.

7. Conclusion

So, first consecration is important, and properly obtaining the pledges and vows; then endeavoring to guard against lapses, and vigorously repairing any root pledge you may have broken in spite of your endeavor. Then, having done that, with pledges and ordination intact, studying, contemplating, and cultivating the mantra path—take this to be the Vajrayāna's vital point. As for meditation on the path, there are two parts: how meditation is done (I will not discuss that here for the time being), and what sort of path you should meditate on.[156] Since this is a place you can go drastically wrong, I will explain exactly what the master Mañjuśrīkīrti has determined in this regard. His *Ornament for the Essence:*

> The great sage Viśvamitra, the knowledge-mantra holder masters Kumārasena, Jayapāda, Ratnamati, and the brahmin Bhadramitra [520], and so forth say the natural purity of all dharmas arises from stopping all wrong thought. Buddha is established through meritorious deeds. Those [who are buddhas-to-be] eliminate ordinary things with the generation stage path and work through the body of forms for the sake of all beings. This is done, by those who become right and perfect buddhas, with the deity's form and unmistaken deeds.

Thus some say the doctrine of emptiness is to be taken up simply to stop wrong thought, because you establish the state of a buddha through the collection of meritorious deeds. Having eliminated ordinary appearances by the generation stage, you work through the body of forms for the sake of living beings. Having become Buddha, with the deity's form and unmistaken deeds you have to establish Buddha. The *Ornament for the Essence:*

> Furthermore the Brahmin Śūnyatābuddhi, the Kāśmīra abbot Prabhāskara, Ānandavajra, the layman Sitikara, the great

> scholar Śrīsiṃha, Vairocanavajra, Hvashang Mahāyānaśrī, Sudattabhadra, the Glorious One with the Blue Lower Robe,[157] Jayapāda, Ratnamati, the brahmin Bhadramitra, and the fully ordained nun Gamo say that statements about a generation stage and deeds are to stop nihilism, and statements about dependent origination establishing dependently originated results [521] are a skillful means, at the start, to look after ordinary persons frightened by profound reality. The right and perfect buddha is inconceivable, nondual transcendental knowledge that is not born from a cause that is incompatible with it. Here there is an emptiness, the non-seeing of a mark, the inconceivable, the complete stopping of elaboration—practitioners, through their mode of intention, in possession of a result that is supreme in the world.

Thus others say that statements about a generation stage and deeds are to stop nihilism, and are a skillful means, at the start, to look after those frightened by profound reality. Buddha is non-conceptual, nondual, transcendental knowledge, not born from an incompatible cause—to wit, conceptual elaboration. So you become a buddha by meditating on a mere emptiness free from elaboration.

Thus these two each are one-sided assertions about becoming a buddha. Taking them as point of departure, the *Ornament for the Essence* goes on to reject them and explain the unmistaken path:[158]

> They have seen just one side, that is, they have not found the path to a right and perfect buddha with certainty. Leave aside their one-sided opinions. Be certain in the knowledge that the supreme vehicle has a philosophical component,[159] the realization free from elaboration, [522] and a praxis component[160] as well—setting forth, step-by-step, into the meditative stabilizations of the generation and completion stages, and setting forth, step-by-step, in reliance on the pledges. Since on this vajra-holder path you directly realize just that[161] and attain the desired good qualities, keep to the steps of the path, cleave to this [path] with the two components.

Thus he says that without veering to a one-sided path you have to have both philosophy and praxis, and that you rely on your pledges and set out, step-by-step, through both the generation and completion [stages]. He has determined, by logic and scriptural citation, what the sacred words of the Buddha in general and the tantras in particular, mean. His is indeed a presentation of the path that captures the imagination of those intelligent and learned ones who desire liberation. So you who are fortunate, set out in this chariot with the two components as fine steeds to pull it, and travel up to the Vajradhara level!

Final Verses

> The glorious Vajrasattva vows are the basis for the siddhis of those who have set out in the Vajrayāna, the supreme revelation of Buddha that produces incomparable delight in the broad-minded. Having read widely about them in the sacred words of the Buddha in general and in the tantras in particular, I have very clearly explained the way you first take them, then keep them, and finally repair them if they are broken.
>
> Obviously those who have rejected the rules of Vajradhara and who say that freedom is acting without care and doing whatever you want to do will not approve of this. I have done it as a mantra party for fortunate and holy students who have lived up to their promise to the buddhas and bodhisattvas to purely carry the great burden of keeping the rules.
>
> The vajraholder's rule is very profound, and I lack the qualifications of wisdom and vigor, so, if faults have crept in here, I reveal them, from my heart, in front of the holy ones.
>
> Now, again, I bow my head to the lotus feet of Lord Mañjuśrī and my teacher. Having gone to them for refuge, even someone like me can probe the profound scriptures a little.
>
> Through the spacelike, vast merit that I have collected here from this work, may all the Buddha's teaching, the single supply of happiness and benefit for living beings, spread everywhere. Having a heartfelt belief in the statement that the teaching alone is the foundation of universal benefit and happiness, may I give joy to the jinas by giving up even my body and life to properly

hold the good Dharma. And may those who are friends also work inexorably, in thought and deed, to hold all the good Dharma of the Victor at all times in order to bring this about.

Colophon

This *Fruit Clusters of Siddhis,* an explanation of the way bodhisattvas following the bodhisattva's way of life by means of secret mantra should make their training in morality completely pure, was requested by many who sincerely want to learn Vajrayāna practices. It was requested by the great Gushri Dondrub Gyelpopa, born into the renowned Dharma Lord Jigten Gonpo's Drigung family line as guide for a vast number of wandering beings, by the great vajra holder learned in the Vidyādhara basket of scriptures Chogowa Tashi Rinchen, and also by my perfect, great spiritual friend, the bilingual Kyabchog Pelzangpo, who understands correctly the vital point of all the sūtras and tantras, has shouldered the burden of the precious doctrine as one, and treats the precious training with the utmost importance and respect. The glorious Śākya bhikṣu, the vajra holder [Tsongkhapa] Lozang Dragpa, having brought together a wide range of tantric scriptures, composed it to the north in the Dragsengzhol mountain hermitage in Reting, in the quiet, distant hermitage of [Dromtonpa] Gyalwe [Jungne].[162] The scribe is Darma Rinchen, a virtuous fellow versed in the three baskets of Buddhist teachings and in the modes of logic and reasoning, who works at his ordination. Based on this, too, may the precious teaching flourish.

Notes

1 The title of Tsongkhapa's talk is *dGe slong gi bslab bya gnam rtser [/rtseng/rtseng] ldeng mar grags*. The written text ends abruptly and is followed by a short note that says the text derives from the notes *(zin bris)* of Tsongkhapa's talk taken by Darma Rinchen. See *Tsong kha pa chen po'i gsung 'bum,* vol. *ka* (Delhi: Ngawang Geleg Demo, 1975), 383.3–6.

2 Earlier in his biography, Khedrub says that Tsongkhapa spent most of the winter and spring of 1400–1401 at Gadong where he gave a series of lectures on Tantric morality, the first mention of this subject. But it is unlikely that Tsongkhapa's *Fruit Clusters of Siddhis* was composed at that time because it contains specific references to his *Basic Path to Awakening.*

3 Mark Tatz, "Asanga's Chapter on Ethics, With the Commentary of Tsong-Kha-Pa, the *Basic Path to Awakening,* the *Complete Bodhisattva,*" in *Studies in Asian Thought and Religion,* vol. IV (Lewiston/Queenston: The Edwin Mellen Press, 1986). The word *gzhung lam,* translated here as "Basic Path," seems to mean "through road," in the sense of having no detours.

4 *Rje tsong kha bas mdzad pa'i byang chub gzhung lam dang rtsa ltung rnam bshad,* and *Rje yab sras kyi gsung rtsom nyer mkho phyogs bsgrigs* (Gansu [Kan su'u zhing]: Mi rigs dpe sgrun khang, 1999).

5 Cyrus Stearns, "The Life and Tibetan Legacy of the Indian Mahāpaṇḍita Vibhūticandra," JIABS (1996) 19.1: 127–68.

6 The words cited are from *rJe btsun bla ma tsong kha pa chen po'i ngo mtshar rmad du byung ba'i rnam par thar pa dad pa'i 'jug ngogs shes bya bya. Tsong kha pa chen po'i gsung 'bum,* vol. *ka* (Delhi: Ngawang Geleg Demo, 1975), 6.2, 137.2, 131.3, and 211.

7 I think it likely that early companions and students of Tsongkhapa like Khedrub understood at least the early Tsongkhapa, and Tsongkhapa's earlier works, among them the *Fruit Clusters,* to have been "in" the Sakya tradition, in the nonexclusive, nonsectarian manner of the time, as did Tsongkhapa himself. It is unlikely that Tsongkhapa and other "proto-Gelug" writers understood themselves as involved in a project defined by making a break from Sakya. When Rongton, and later Gorampa (1429–89) and Shakya Chogden (1428–1507), insisted that Tsongkhapa's views constituted a radical departure from a received, earlier Sakya tradition, this sharpened a divide. An early Gandenpa entity then projected Tsongkhapa as the founder of a new sect.

8 Max Nihom, *The Kuñjarakarṇadharmakathana and the Yogatantra.* Publications of the De Nobili Research Library, vol. XXI (Vienna, 1994), p. 9. Nihom's comment that there is a disconnect between systems of thought that become ever more rarified and, in course of time, seem to be inadequate to the direct experience that is defining of the pop or mass cultures in which, in some inexplicable way, the elite

literature seems to have originated at least suggests the beginning of an explanation of the very confusing mix of the elite and popular in tantra.

9 It should be noted that this *Vajra Tip Tantra* is not the *Vajra Tip Tantra (Vajraśekharatantra)* well known to Japanese Buddhism (Shingon), but an explanation yoga tantra connected with the *Compendium of Principles Tantra (Tattvasaṃgraha)*. In Japan, the *Vajra Tip Tantra (Vajraśekharatantra)* is the *Compendium of Principles Tantra (Tattvasaṃgraha)* itself. The Tibetan *Vajra Tip Tantra (rGyud rdo rje tse mo)* appears not to have been translated into Japanese.

10 Paul Williams, *Buddhist Thought: A Complete Introduction to the Indian Tradition* (London: Routledge, 2000), and Anthony Tribe, "Mañjuśrī and *The Chanting of the Names of Mañjuśrī (Nāmasaṅgīti)*: Wisdom and Its Embodiment in an Indian Mahāyāna Buddhist Text," in *Indian Insights: Buddhism, Brahmanism and Bhakti*, Peter Connolly and Sue Hamilton, eds. (London: Luzac Oriental, 1997), pp. 109–36, point out that the term highest yoga tantra is used loosely and sometimes anachronistically by Tibetans. For convenience the Tibetan system as set forth in Lessing and Wayman's Mkhas grub rje's *Fundamentals of the Buddhist Tantras*, Indo-Iranian Monographs, vol. VIII (The Hague: Mouton: 1968) and Jeffrey Hopkins's *Tantra in Tibet and Yoga in Tibet* (London: Allen and Unwin, 1980, 1982) is accepted here.

11 Cyrus Stearns, *The Buddha from Dolpo* (Albany: State University of New York Press, 1999).

12 *Bla ma lnga bcu ba'i rnam bshad slob ma'i re ba kun skong*, in Gareth Sparham, *Fulfillment of All Hopes* (Boston: Wisdom Publications, 2000).

13 Anthony Tribe, in "Mañjuśrī and *The Chanting of the Names of Mañjuśrī*" (p. 129, n. 29), says the following about *jñāna* (the Sanskrit *jñ* is cognate with the *gn* in "gnosis" and the *kn* in "know"). "I use the word 'Knowledge' to render *jñāna*...I prefer 'Awareness' in that it emphasises *jñāna*'s experiential or subjective pole...For *advayajñāna* and *pañca jñānāni* I have consistently used 'Awareness' (thus 'Nondual Awareness' and 'the five Awarenesses'). Elsewhere, and outside of these more technical uses of *jñāna*, I have also relied on 'wisdom' as a translation."

14 Alexander Cunningham, writing in 1853, *Ladāk Physical, Statistical and Historical* (New Delhi: Sagar Publications, 1970), 363–64, citing B. H. Hodgson, *Essays on the Languages, Literature and Religion of Nepal and Tibet*, reprint edition, (Varanasi: Bharat-Bharati, 1971).

15 Richard Gombrich, "Organized Bodhisattvas: A Blind Alley in Buddhist Historiography," in *Sūryacandrāya Essays in Honour of Akira Yuyama on the Occasion of His 65th Birthday*, Paul Harrison and Gregory Schopen, eds. (Swisttal-Odendorf, 1998), pp. 45–56.

16 *sems can gyi khams* (Skt: *sattvadhātu*) might mean the place that living beings inhabit.

17 *Vajrayāna Root Downfalls*, 5ab.

18 *Vajrayāna Root Downfalls*, 5cd.

19 *Vajrayāna Root Downfalls*, 6ab.

20 *Vajrayāna Root Downfalls*, 8ab.

21 *Vajrayāna Root Downfalls*, 8cd–9ab.

22 Enlightenment is the supreme, unshared siddhi. The shared siddhis include the ability to fly or plunge into the earth unhindered, to know a certain number of a person's past and future lives, to hear distant sounds, to read minds, and so on.

23 Extracts from the *Vajra Tip Tantra* are from the *Co ne* edition (printed to order

by the *Shes rab phar khang,* Dharmsala, n.d.), the only edition available to me when I first worked on the text. The principal section begins abruptly on page 764 with "...also the inquiry: To accomplish the knowledge-continuum how are the vows taken? How are the pledges protected? How do they degenerate?" The section ends on page 770 with the statement *rdo rje slob dpon gyi las rdzogs so.* This section is located within a larger subdivision of the text starting on page 754 that is called the *Drawing Closer (dgug pa) of the Total Enlightenment of the Buddhas Within the Secret Maṇḍala of All Tathāgatas.* This again falls within the second part *(le'u)* of the *Vś* (pp. 680–776) called *Setting Forth into the Vast Ways of Enlightenment (Byang chub pa'i tshul rgya chen pos 'jug pa).*

24 *śuddha:* "pure" instead of *śubha:* "beautiful."

25 Nagpochopa could render Kṛṣṇacarya, and Nagpopa could render Kṛṣṇapāda, Kanhā, etc. I have left the name untranslated because it is not certain.

26 "seal," "partner," or "hand gesture."

27 Śāntipa usually renders Ratnākaraśānti, but again it is uncertain, so I have left the name untranslated. His commentary is the *Śrīguhyasamājamaṇḍalavidhiṭīkā.* Dīpaṃkarabhadra's *Guhyasamāja Maṇḍala Ritual* in four hundred and fifty lines is the *Śrīguhyasamājamaṇḍalavidhi.* The Tibetan abbreviation comes from the statement at the end of the text "...four hundred and fifty lines of verse" *(...sho lo ka bzhi brgya lnga bcu),* D.T. Suzuki, ed., *The Tibetan Tripitaka: Peking Edition* (Tokyo: Kyoto, 1961) [hereafter referred to by the abbreviation P], 2728:45.5.8.

28 pledge: *samaya;* also translated as "commitment" or "relationship."

29 vow: *saṃvara;* also translated as "ordination" or "restraint."

30 The three vehicles intended here are the Listener, Pratyekabuddha, and Bodhisattva vehicles, and the "and so forth" incorporates the two external lower tantra sets and two secret higher tantra sets.

31 An interlinear note in Buton's *rDo rje thams cad 'byung ba'i rgya cher bshad pa yid bzhin nor bu zhes bya ba* says that Nyen is the holder of this view. See *The Collected Works of Bu ston,* L. Chandra, ed., vol. 11, 185–832 (Delhi: International Academy of Indian Culture, 1967), p. 754.4.

32 The three not mentioned are not to steal, not to lie, and not to fornicate.

33 "And so forth" refers to giving up supporting living beings, forsaking one's retinue, and being attached to nirvāṇa.

34 I have been unable to identify this work.

35 That is, highest yoga tantras may or may not announce all the unique pledges, shared vows unique to yoga and highest yoga tantra, and more basic moralities shared in common with all bodhisattvas and spiritual beings in general. Some only give a few, while assuming implicit understanding of all, and some give the complete set.

36 This is the tentative position taken by Buton in *Yid bzhin nor bu,* 754.7, who says that Nyen's position "appears to accord with these citations."

37 *dza landha ra.*

38 This Tibetan seems to be a different translation of the name of the same text that Tsongkhapa explains in detail (439.2ff).

39 There are a number of names for this tantra: *Saṃbhuṭa, Saṃpuṭa,* and *Saṃpuṭi* among them.

40 The *Vajra Tip Tantra* is a yoga tantra and the other two are highest yoga tantras. Tsongkhapa misleadingly calls the *Ḍākārṇava Yoginī Tantra rDo rje mkha' 'gro,*

even though he calls Bhavabhadra's *Commentary on the Vajraḍāka Tantra (Śrīvajraḍāka-nāma-mahātantrarājasya vivṛtti) rDo rje mkha' 'gro'i 'grel pa. Ḍākārṇava Yoginī Tantra* renders *Śrīḍākārṇavamahāyoginītantrarāja-nāma* P19:107.3.3–4.1.

41 This is the view of Dragpa Gyeltsen, in *rTsa ba'i ltung ba bcu bzhi pa'i 'grel pa gsal byed 'khrul pa spong ba,* in *Sa skya pa'i bka' 'bum,* vol. 3 (Tokyo: Toyo Bunko, 1968), pp. 235–265.3. See Mark Tatz, *Candragomin's Twenty Verses on the Bodhisattva Vow and Its Commentary* (Dharmsala: Library of Tibetan Works and Archives, 1982), p. 34.

42 *sbyor ba.*

43 *rnal sbyor pa.*

44 *sems can gyi khams (sattvadhātu)* might possibly mean the place that living beings inhabit.

45 403.1 emend *bla* to *sla.*

46 Some versons read *yang* in place of *brgyad.*

47 *brahmavihāras.*

48 lit., "whose accomplishment is not in vain."

49 *gtong sems.*

50 Even given the different interpretations of these lines, the text as it stands hardly makes sense. The original was something like *bāhyaguhyayānatraya.* VŚ 769.5 reads *las* for *la* in the first line and in the third line reads *phyi nang gsang ba'i theg pa gsum* in place of 412.5 *phyi dang gsang ba theg pa gsum.*

51 *mtshan nyid theg pa, *lakṣaṇayāna.* I understand the name for this vehicle to refer to the scriptures that give the particular and general characteristics *(lakṣaṇa)* of the basic elements of Buddhism.

52 *chos 'di pa.*

53 I am unsure how to render the exact reading *mchod pa byas nan tan ye shes,* though the sense is clear enough. I have taken *byas (bya bas)* to be the Sanskrit *iti.*

54 This might be a paraphrase of P2328:154.5.2–6 rather than an alternative translation. In place of *sa bon* 154.5.2 read *khu ba.*

55 In the consecration rite of throwing a flower into the maṇḍala and seeing where it lands.

56 Although only the one *Viṃśati* ("Twenty") maṇḍala ritual of Nāgabodhi is listed in the P catalogue (the *Guhyasamāja Maṇḍala Ritual* cited above), in his *List of Texts Received* (*gSen yig, Tsong kha pa chen po'i gsung 'bum* [Collected Works], vol. *ka* [Delhi: Ngawang Geleg Demo, 1975], 235.1), Tsongkhapa seems to be referring to these two maṇḍala rituals by Nāgabodhi when he says: *cho ga nyi shu ti la ka ka la sha/ pa tshab kyi 'gyur/ 'di g[n]yis klu byang gis mdzad.*

57 This part of the maṇḍala ritual consecration is in the *nang 'jug* ("entering in") section. The disciple enters from the east, circumambulates, and bows to the diety, then, in the *dam bzhag byed pa* ("giving solemn promise") section, requests ordination. In the *dam ye dbyer med* ("pledge and wisdom being indivisible") and *brten pa* ("fixing [the resolve]") sections they give their word as a pledge and are given garlands.

58 *bdag po.*

59 Buton, *Yid bzhin nor bu,* 757.4, says in an interlinear note that Lama Chophag holds this view.

60 *Dkyil chog yon tan kun 'byung* may be the name of an unidentified maṇḍala

ritual. If so, this would be rendered "As in the *Guṇasamudaya/sambhava*(?) *Maṇḍala Ritual,* the production of the thought of Buddha's enlightenment."

61 Compare this with the use of *mtha' rten* ("boundary base") below.

62 *mtha' rten.*

63 *gsung bgros.*

64 Compare the four set forth by in Tatz, *Candragomin's Twenty Verses on the Bodhisattva Vow,* pp. 41–42.

65 *rtsa ba nas chad par mi 'gyur ba.*

66 *dbang za ba.*

67 *bla mas* to *bla ma'i?*

68 *Mdor byas pa'i 'grel pa rin phreng.* I have not been able to conclusively identify this text, so the translation is tentative.

69 *sarvavajravrata.*

70 Tatz, *Basic Path to Awakening,* pp. 67ff.

71 P3961:122.1.7–8. That this is a contentious issue is evident from Dragpa Gyeltsen's long refutation of wrong views at the opening of his *rTsa ba'i ltung ba bcu bzhi pa'i 'grel pa.*

72 "Root downfall" renders the Sanskrit *mūlāpatti* and "gross downfall" *sthūlāpatti.*

73 "Indestructible Vehicle."

74 "Indestructible Being."

75 *karmāvaraṇa.*

76 This is a creative etymology of *āpatti* from the Sanskrit root *pat,* "to fall," and from the root *pad,* "to produce."

77 This is the view of Dragpa Gyeltsen in *rTsa ba'i ltung ba bcu bzhi pa'i 'grel pa* 242.4.6, explaining in brief 236.4.1–2.

78 *ltung ba'i rtsa ba.*

79 *rgyud.*

80 *rgyun.*

81 I have been unable to identify this work.

82 Perhaps this finds *ācārya* in *hitecchā* and *amatsārya.*

83 I have changed the Tibetan ka° to kā° here and elsewhere.

84 *Guhyasamaja-Tantra,* ed. B. Bhatatacharyya (Baroda: Gaekward Oriental Series, 1931), 15, 4–5ab.

85 The reading is uncertain. Tsongkhapa's comment at 444.2 *de spangs na rtsa ltung du 'gro* suggests emending *ma spangs* to *spangs:* "They forsake them. Having forsaken, it is a root downfall."

86 Tatz, *Basic Path to Awakening,* p. 65, renders this passage from the *Bodhisattva Levels,* "...a greater degree of involvement—by which the bodhisattva makes a regular practice...generates not the slightest sense of shame and embarassment, is pleased with and glad of it, and has a view for its good qualities. This should be understood as greater involvement." Tsongkhapa (Tatz, *Basic Path to Awakening,* p. 194), says "non-production of conscience and lack of concern for the disadvantages" (two absences) and "desire to do it in future and being pleased with and glad of it" (two presences) are necessary for greater involvement. A sense of shame or concern for the disadvantages preclude the absences the moment they arise, hence must be absent for the entire duration. "The two presences should develop at some point during that period." See also Tatz, *Candragomin's Twenty Verses on the Bodhisattva Vow,* p. 39.

87 In Akhu Sherab Gyatso's list of rare books *(Tho yig)* his name is given as mGos Khug-pa lHas-btsas-dbang-phyug-rgya-mtsho. His clan name is 'Gos and place name Khug-pa.

88 A paraphrase of P3314:3.4.8–5.1. Is this the *Long Commentary (rGya cher 'grel pa)* that Dragpa Gyeltsen attacks at the start of his *rTsa ba'i ltung ba bcu bzhi pa'i 'grel pa*? He denies this commentary attributed to Mañjuśrīkīrti is actually written by him.

89 *pārājika.*

90 It is a peculiarity of this text (e.g., 446.4, 454.5, 457.2, 462.2) that *dka' 'grel* (Skt: *pañjikā*) is written *bka' 'grel.*

91 *saṃghāvaśeṣa.*

92 The translation of *shan 'dra* and of *dag* (–> *drag*?) is conjectural.

93 "Those gone to excellence," "excellently gone," "from whom it is excellently gone."

94 Dragpa Gyeltsen, *rTsa ba'i ltung ba bcu bzhi pa'i 'grel pa,* 243–45. The *Bodhisattva Levels* (in Tatz, *Basic Path to Awakening,* p. 64) says, "There are four events that function in likeness to [Prātimokṣa grounds for defeat]." The prātimokṣa defeats are murder, theft, lying about high spiritual attainment, and sexual intercourse. Tsongkhapa (ibid., p. 163) says the four are eight, "The statement that the defeats are four is made in the face of attitude. So there are four defeats of (1) attachment to gain and respect, (2) stinginess in goods, (3) thoughts of harm towards sentient beings, and (4) the stupidity of abusing the doctrine. They are eight, on the other hand, in view of their application. So there are defeats of (1–2) praising oneself and deprecating another, (3–4) not giving doctrine and not giving wealth, (5–6) striking sentient beings and not accepting an apology, and (7–8) rejecting the good doctrine and teaching a semblance of the doctrine."

95 This is the first meaning of *sun 'byin pa* in S.C. Das's *A Tibetan-English Dictionary* [reprint edition] (New Delhi: Gaurav Publishing House, 1985).

96 "frequenters of the river banks."

97 *sun 'byin.*

98 Tatz, *Basic Path to Awakening,* p. 77 (*Bodhisattva Levels* 79b1): "If he has no inclination but does not repudiate them either, there is no fault."

99 *Ornament for the Mahāyāna Sūtras* 1.21, *Jewel Garland* 5.88a–89b as cited by Tatz, *Basic Path for Awakening,* p. 231, fn. 477.

100 Contra Dragpa Gyeltsen, *rTsa ba'i ltung ba bcu bzhi pa'i 'grel pa,* 250.2.5.

101 *rje gnang.*

102 *slang* to *spang*?

103 Tsongkhapa does not seem to count this as a work separate from the *Clusters of Quintessential Instructions*. He refers to both as *Man ngag snye ma.*

104 The English translation of this, and the following Tibetan translations, are all speculative in the absence of an original.

105 At the conclusion of the commentary attributed to Lakṣmīṅkara (P3311) it says the vows "have been drawn from the *Fifty Stanzas on the Guru.*"

106 *bas* to *las*?

107 I do not understand what this means.

108 I have been unable to identify this commentary that Tsongkhapa calls *'Ggrel pa bdud rtsi'i chu rgyun*. It is not in the list of codifications of morality compiled by T. Skorupski in his "Vajrayāna Offenses" (unpublished paper, 2003). I thank Dr. Skorupski for allowing me to make use of his list.

109 Dragpa Gyeltsen in *rTsa ba'i ltung ba bcu bzhi pa'i 'grel pa* reads *dam tshig rdzas ni ji bzhin rnyed*...in Mā 8c.

110 There is a short *Kāmaśāstra* in the P catalogue that appears to be a summary of Vātsyāyana's sūtras.

111 By Padmasaṃbhavapāda in the P catalogue; Padmavajra according to Dragpa Gyeltsen, *rTsa ba'i ltung ba bcu bzhi pa'i 'grel pa,* 256.4.

112 In the sense of "consort."

113 I am not certain what *shan 'dra ru mdzas* means.

114 Brahmeśvara-sampanna.

115 "One Who Puts on a Show."

116 *rang bzhin pa.*

117 Both this and the following citation from the *Five Pledges* are found in Dragpa Gyeltsen's *rTsa ba'i ltung ba bcu bzhi pa'i 'grel pa,* 235.3.4–5. Saroruhavajra wrote a *Guhyakośa-nāma-mantraśāstra* (P 4699).

118 The entire text is translated by Jan-Ulrich Sobisch in his *Three-Vow Theories in Tibetan Buddhism* (Wiesbaden: Dr. Ludwig Reichert, 2002).

119 Māra is a god who comes in a guise similar to the Buddha to hinder those at a high stage of spiritual development.

120 The translation is conjectural.

121 *kun man da* to *ku-mandāra*?

122 *sngon* to *mngon.*

123 Emend *'khu bar byed* to *khru bar byed* (484.5).

124 explanation tantras and their subexplanations.

125 *nag por bshad pa* and *chen por ston pa.*

126 The four seals sealing a doctrine as Buddhist are well known. I do not know what the three seals are, unless they are the seals that come when a scripture has been subjected to the three stages of examination exemplified by examining, washing, and scraping gold nuggets. *do ka-shi* must be rendering some form of *dhāv* and *kaṣ*. This statement attributed to the Buddha is much cited.

127 Emend °*de nyid gsal*° to *'di nyid*° (487.5).

128 Tatz, *Basic Path to Awakening,* p. 83.

129 As explained in Tatz, *Basic Path to Awakening,* p. 183.

130 I have not been able to identify this text.

131 The third subdivision of the path of preparation *(prayogamārga)* according to Vasubandhu.

132 Although the general meaning is clear enough, some words seem to be missing from the Tibetan text at this point.

133 This text is not in the P catalogue.

134 Dragpa Gyeltsen, *rTsa ba'i ltung ba bcu bzhi pa'i 'grel pa,* 241.1.1–5. See Tatz, *Basic Path to Awakening,* pp. 241–42.

135 Statues, holy texts, and members of the community.

136 *tsha tsha.*

137 The P catalogue lists *Vajra Tent Tantra Commentaries* by Kṛṣṇapāda, Indrabodhi, and Devakulamahāmati.

138 Perhaps a misprint for *snying po zhabs,* i.e., Ānandagarbha.

139 505.2 has *bshad* ("are said to be") in place of *brgyad.*

140 *vrata.*

141 *rim pas so* to *rim pas.*

142 Cf. 458–59.

143 There are five commentaries on the *Five Stages* listed in the P catalogue, 2696–2700.
144 "driven being."
145 *bshad* to *brgyad* as at 500.3.
146 *bsnyen.*
147 *bdag gis* to *bdag nyid?*
148 "serpent spirit."
149 "furious gods."
150 *bas* to *las.*
151 *myung gnas.*
152 *dbang gi* to *dbang gis?*
153 In other words, make them feel bad about what they are doing.
154 *maithunā.*
155 *shed khyer byas.*
156 Tsongkhapa evidently already had it in mind to compose his *Great Exposition of Tantra (sNgags rim chen mo)* at this point.
157 *dpal sham thabs sngon po can.*
158 Compare this with the two extremes *(khyab che ba* and *khyab cung ba)* in the Insight *(lhag stong chen mo)* section of the *Lam rim chen mo,* written at about the same time.
159 *lta ba'i tshul.*
160 *spyod pa'i tshul.*
161 *de nyid.*
162 *rgyal ba'i dben gnas kyi yang dgon.*

Outline of the Text

Table of Names

Abhayākara Abhayākaragupta	a-bhya-ka-ra/a-bhya
Akhu Sherab Gyatso	A-khu Shes-rab-rgya-mtsho
Ānandagarbha	Kun-dga'-snying-po/Kun-snying
Ānandavajra	Ā-nanta-bajra
Ar Changchub Yeshey	'Ar Byang-chub-ye-shes
Aśvaghoṣa	rTa-dbyangs
Bhadramitra	bZang-po'i-gshen-gnyen
Bhāvabhadra	Bhā-va-bha-tra
Bhavyakīrti	sKal-ldan-grags-pa
[Buddha]-jñāna-pāda	[Sangs-rgyas] Ye-shes-zhabs
Buton	Bu-ston Rin-chen-grub
Candrabhadra	Zla-ba-bzang-po
Chogowa Tashi Rinchen	Chos-sgo-ba bKra-shis-rin-chen
Chokyi Lodro	Chos-kyi-blo-gros
Dārikapa	Dā-ri-ka-pa
Darma Rinchen	Dar-ma-rin-chen
Dīpaṃkarabhadra	Mar-me-mdzas-bzang-po
Dolpopa	Dol-po-pa Shes-rab-rgyal-mtshan
Dragpa Gyelsten	Grags-pa-rgyal-mtshan
Dragsengzhol	Brag-seng-ge'i-zhol
Drigung	'Bri-gung
Drigung Kagyu	'Bri-gung bKa'-brgyud
Dromtonpa Gyalwe Jungne	'Brom-ston-pa rGyal-ba'i-byung-gnas

Dungkar Lozang Tinley	Dung-dkar bLo-bzang-'phrin-las
Gadong	dGa'-gdong
Gamo	dGa'-mo
Ganden Potrang	dGa'-ldan-po-brang
Gandenpa	dGa'-ldan-pa
Gendundrub	dGe-gdun-grub
Gorampa	Go-rab-'byams-pa bSod-nams-seng-ge
Gushri Dondrub Gyelpopa	Gu-śrī Don-grub-rgyal-po-pa
Hvashang Mahāyānaśrī	dGe-slong Theg-chen-dpal
Jayabhadra	rGyal-ba-bzang-po
Jayapāda	rGyal-ba'i-zhabs
Je Rinpoche Go Khugpa Lhachay	rJe Rin-po-che 'Gos Khug-pa-lhas-gce
Jetsun Sakyapa	rJe-btsun Sa-skya-pa [Grags-pa-rgyal-mtshan]
Jigten Gonpo	'Jig-rten-mgon-po
Jowo Chenpo	Jo-bo-chen-po
Kadam	bKa-gdams
Kāśmīra	Kha-che
Khedrub	mKhas-grub dPal-bzang-po
Konchog Sum	dKon-mchog-gsum
Kumaracandra	gZhon-nu-zla-ba
Kumārasena	gZhon-nu'i-sde
Kyabchog Pelzangpo	sKyab-mchog dPal-bzang-po
Lama Chophag	bLa-ma Chos-'phags
Lawapa	Lwa-ba-pa
Lozang Dragpa	bLo-bzang-grags-pa
Mañjuśrī	'Jam-pa'i-dbyangs
Mañjuśrīkīrti	'Jam-dpal-grags-pa
Munendrabhadra	Mu-nendra-bha-tra

Nāgabodhi	kLu-byang
Nāgārjuna	kLu-grub
Nagpo Damtsigdorje	Nag-po-dam-tshig-rdo-rje (Kṛṣṇa Samayavajra)
Nagpochopa	Nag-po-spyod-pa
Nagpopa	Nag-po-pa
Nagtso	Nag-tsho
Namtsedeng	gNam-rtser-ldeng
Namtsedengma	gNam-rtser-ldeng-ma
Nandivajra	dGa-ba'i-rdo-rje
Nyen	gNyan
Nyingmapa	rNying-ma-pa
Padmāṅkuśa	Padma-lcags-kyu
Prabhāskara	Rab-snang-byed-pa
Rahulaśrīmitra	sGra-gcan-'dzin-dpal-gzhes-gnyen
Ratnamati	Rin-chen-ldan
Rendawa	Red-mda'-ba
Reting	Rva-sgreng
Rongton	Rong-ston Śākya-rgyal-mtshan-dpal-bzang-po/Shes-bya-kun-rig
Sakya	Sa-skya
Sakya Pandita	Sa-skya paṇḍi-ta Kun-dga'-rgyal-mtshan
Saraha	Sa-ra-ha
Saroruha	mTsho-skyes
Shakya Chogden	gSer-ldog-paṇ-chen Śākya-mchog-ldan
Sitikara	Si-ti-ka-ra
Śrīdhara	dPal-'dzin
Śrīsiṃha	dDal-gyi-seng-ge
Sudattabhadra	Legs-sbyin-bzang-po

Śūnyatābuddhi	sTong-nyid-blo
Temochen	lTad-mo-can
Tsangpa Punsumtsogpa Wangchug	Tsang-pa-phun-sum-tshogs-pa-dbang-phyug (Brahmeśvara-saṃpanna)
Tselpa Kungadorje	Tshal-pa Kun-dga'-rdo-rje
Tsongkhapa	Tsong-kha-pa
Udbhaṭa Suraṅga	mTho-btsun-btso-legs
Vāgīśvarakīrti	Ngag-dbang-grags-pa
Vairocanavajra	sNang-mdzad-rdo-rje
Vajrasaṃnāha	rDo-rje-go-cha
Vibhūticandra	Bi-bhūtī-tsa-ntra
Vimalagupta	Dri-med-sbas-pa
Viśvamitra	Bi-shva-mi-tra
Yarlung	Yar-klung

Bibliography

Bhatatacharyya, Benoytosh, ed. 1931. *Guhyasamāja-Tantra or Tathāgata Guhyaka.* Gaekward Oriental Series 53. Baroda.

Bu-ston Rin-chen-grub. 1967. *Rdo rje thams cad 'byung ba'i rgya cher bshad pa yid bzhin nor bu zhes bya ba.* In *The Collected Works of Bu ston*, vol. 11, pp. 185–832. L. Chandra, ed. Delhi: International Academy of Indian Culture.

Cozort, Daniel G. 1986. *Highest Yoga Tantra.* Ithaca: Snow Lion Publications.

Cunningham, Alexander. 1970 [1853]. *Ladāk Physical, Statistical and Historical.* New Delhi: Sagar Publications.

Das, S. C. 1985. *A Tibetan-English Dictionary.* Reprinted from the first edition. [Calcutta, 1902]. New Delhi: Gaurav Publishing House.

Eastman, K. W. 1981. "The Eighteen Tantras of the Vajraśekhara/Māyājāla." Paper presented to the 26th International Conference of Orientalists in Japan. Tokyo, May 8.

Gombrich, R. F. 1998. "Organized Bodhisattvas: A Blind Alley in Buddhist Historiography." In *Sūryacandrāya Essays in Honour of Akira Yuyama on the Occasion of His 65th Birthday,* pp. 45–56. Paul Harrison and Gregory Schopen, eds. Swisttal-Odendorf: Indica et Tibetica.

Grags-pa-rgyal-mtshan. 1968. *Rtsa ba'i ltung ba bcu bzhi pa'i 'grel pa gsal byed 'khrul pa spong ba.* In *Sa skya pa'i bka' 'bum,* vol. 3, pp. 235–265.3. Tokyo: Toyo Bunko.

Gyurme Dorje. 1991. "The rNying-ma Interpretation of Commitment and Vow." *The Buddhist Forum,* 2: 71–95.

Hakuju et al., eds. 1997. *Complete Catalogue of the Tibetan Buddhist Canons (Bkah-hgyur and Bstan-hgyur).* Derge edition. Sendai: Tohoku Imperial University.

Harvey, Peter. 2000. *An Introduction to Buddhist Ethics*. New York: Cambridge University Press.

Hodgson, B. H. 1971 [1874]. *Essays on the Languages, Literature and Religion of Nepal and Tibet*. Reprint edition. Varanasi: Bharat-Bharati.

Hopkins, Jeffrey. 1980. *Tantra in Tibet*. London: Allen and Unwin.

———. 1982. *Yoga in Tibet*. London: Allen and Unwin.

Jackson, D. 1989.*The Early Abbots of 'Phan po Na-lendra: The Vicissitudes of a Great Tibetan Monastery in the Fifteenth Century*. Vienna: Arbeitskreis für Tibetische und Buddhistische Studien, Universität Wien.

Keown, Damien. 1992. *The Nature of Buddhist Ethics*. London: Macmillan Press.

———. 1995. *Buddhism and Bioethics*. New York: St. Martin's Press.

Kongtrul Lodro Taye, Jamgon. 1998. *Buddhist Ethics*. Ed. and trans. by the International Translation Committee founded by V.V. Kalu Rinpoche. Ithaca: Snow Lion Publications.

Lessing, Ferdinand D., and Alex Wayman eds. and trans. 1968. *Mkhas grub rje's Fundamentals of the Buddhist Tantras*. Indo-Iranian Monographs, vol. VIII. The Hague: Mouton.

Lévi, S. 1929. "Autour d'Aśvaghoṣa." JA (Oct–Dec): 266–67.

Matsunaga, Yukei. 1977. "A History of Tantric Buddhism in India with Reference to Chinese Translations." In *Buddhist Thought and Asian Civilization*, pp. 167–181. Leslie S. Kawamura and Keith Scott, eds. Emeryville, California: Dharma Publishing.

mKhas-grub Ge-legs dPal-bzang-po. 1975. *Rje btsun bla ma tsong kha pa chen po'i ngo mtshar rmad du byung ba'i rnam par thar pa dad pa'i 'jug ngogs shes bya bya. Tsong kha pa chen po'i gsung 'bum* [Collected Works of Tsongkhapa], vol. ka. Delhi: Ngawang Geleg Demo.

———. 1999. *Sdom pa gsum kyi rnam par bzhag pa mdor bsdus te gtan la dbab pa'i rab tu byed pa thub bstan rin po che'i byi dor*. In *Rje yab sras kyi gsung rtsom nyer mkho phyogs bsgrigs*. Gansu (Kan su'u zhing): Mi rigs dpe sgrun khang. Distributed by mTsho sngon zhing chen zhin hwa dpe khang and printed by Zi ling mi rigs par khang.

Ngari Panchen Pema Wangyi Gyalpo. 1996. *Perfect Conduct: Ascertaining the Three Vows*. Commentary by His Holiness Dudjom Rinpoche. Khenpo

Gyurme Samdrub and Sangye Khandro, trans. Boston: Wisdom Publications.

Nihom, Max. 1994. *The Kuñjarakarṇadharmakathana and the Yogatantra*. Publications of the De Nobili Research Library, vol. XXI. Vienna.

Reigle, David. 1983.*The Books of Kiu-te or The Tibetan Buddhist Tantras*. San Diego: Wizards Bookshelf.

Rhoton, Jared Douglas, trans. 2002. *A Clear Differentiation of the Three Codes*. Albany: State University of New York Press.

Ruegg, David Seyfort. 1989. *Buddha-nature, Mind, and the Problem of Gradualism in a Comparative Perspective: On the Transmission and Reception of Buddhism in India and Tibet*. London: School of Oriental and African Studies, University of London.

Sa-skya paṇḍi-ta Kun-dga'-rgyal-mtshan. 2002. *Phyogs thams cad las rnam par rgyal ba chen po 'jam mgon sa skya paṇḍi ta kun dga' rgyal mtshan dpal bzang po'i zhabs kyi gsung rab glegs bam gsum pa las sdom pa gsum gyi rab tu dbye ba'i bstan bcos*. In Jared Douglas Rhoton, *A Clear Differentiation of the Three Codes*. Albany: State University of New York Press.

Sizemore, Russell F., and Donald K. Swearer, eds. *Ethics, Wealth, and Salvation*. Columbia: University of South Carolina.

Skorupski, T. 2003. "Vajrayāna Offenses." Unpublished paper.

Snellgrove, David. 1959. *The Hevajra Tantra*. London Oriental Series 6. London.

Sobisch, Jan-Ulrich. 1997. "Preliminary Remarks on the Three-Vow Theories *(sdom pa gsum)* of Tibetan Buddhism." *Tibetan Studies* (Proceedings of the 7th Seminar of the IATS, Graz 1995), vol. 2, pp. 891–902. Wien: Verlag der Osterreichishen Akademie der Wissenschaftern.

———. 2002. *Three-Vow Theories in Tibetan Buddhism*. Wiesbaden: Dr. Ludwig Reichert.

Sparham, Gareth. 2000. *The Fulfillment of All Hopes: Guru Devotin in Tibetan Buddhism*. Boston: Wisdom Publications.

Stearns, Cyrus. 1996. "The Life and Tibetan Legacy of the Indian Mahāpaṇḍita Vibhūticandra." JIABS 19.1: 127–168.

———. 1999. *The Buddha from Dolpo*. Albany: State University of New York Press.

Steinkellner, Ernst. 1978. "Remarks on Tantristic Hermeneutics." In *Proceedings of the Csoma de Korös Memorial Symposium,* vol. XXIII, pp. 445–458. L. Ligeti, ed. Bibliotheca Orientalis Hungarica. Budapest: Akadémiai Kiadó.

Strickmann, Michel. 1977. "A Survey of Tibetan Buddhist Studies." *Eastern Buddhist,* 10.1: 128–149.

Suzuki, D. T., ed. 1961. *The Tibetan Tripitaka: Peking Edition.* Tokyo: Kyoto.

Tatz, Mark. 1982. *Candragomin's Twenty Verses on the Bodhisattva Vow and Its Commentary.* Dharmsala: Library of Tibetan Works and Archives.

———. 1986. *Asanga's Chapter on Ethics, With the Commentary of Tsong-Kha-pa, the Basic Path to Awakening, the Complete Bodhisattva.* Studies in Asian Thought and Religion, vol. IV. Lewiston/Queenston: The Edwin Mellen Press.

Tribe, Anthony. 1997. "Mañjuśrī and *The Chanting of the Names of Mañjuśrī (Nāmasaṅgīti):* Wisdom and Its Embodiment in an Indian Mahāyāna Buddhist text." In *Indian Insights: Buddhism, Brahmanism and Bhakti,* pp. 109–136. Peter Connolly and Sue Hamilton, eds. London: Luzac Oriental.

Tsong-kha-pa bLo-bzang-grags-pa. 1975. *Dge tshul gyi bslab bya gnam rtsed ldeng ma* and *dGe slong gi bslab bya gnam rtsed ldeng mar grags* pa (collectively known as *Rnam rtsed ldeng ma*). *Byang chub sems dpa'i tshul khrims kyi rnam bshad byang chub gzhung lam. Gsang sngags kyi tshul khrims kyi rnam bshad dngos grub kyi snye ma. Gsen yig. Tsong kha pa chen po'i gsung 'bum* [Collected Works], vol. ka. Delhi: Ngawang Geleg Demo.

———. 2000. *Bla ma lnga bcu ba'i rnam bshad slob ma'i re ba kun skong.* In Sparham, 2000.

Williams, Paul. 2000. *Buddhist Thought: A Complete Introduction to the Indian Tradition.* London: Routledge.

Works Cited by Tsongkhapa

These are works cited in *rTsa ltung rnam bshad.* Titles as they are rendered within the English translation are followed, in the case of Indian works, by the title given in the catalogue to the *Tibetan Tripitaka Peking Edition* (ed. D.T. Suzuki, 1961) and, in the case of works in Tibetan, by the title where it could be ascertained.

Ākāśagarbha Sūtra, Āryākāśagarbha-nāma-mahāyānasūtra

All Secrets Tantra, Sarvarahasya-nāma-tantra

Basic Path of Awakening, Byang chub gzhung lam

Bhūtaḍāmara Tantra, Bhūtaḍāmaramahātantrarāja

Black Yamāri Maṇḍala Ritual, Kṛṣṇayamārimaṇḍalopāyikā

Black Yamāri Tantra, Sarvatathāgatakāyavākcittakṛṣṇayamāri-nāma-tantra

Bodhisattva Levels, Bodhisattva-bhūmi

Bounteous Array Sūtra, Ghanavyūhasūtra

Buddha Kapāla Maṇḍala Ritual, Śrībuddhakapāla-nāma-maṇḍalavidhikrama-pradyotana

Buddhakapāla Tantra, Śrībuddhakapāla-nāma-yoginītantrarāja

Clarification of Union Maṇḍala Ritual, Yuganaddhaprakāśa-nāma-sekaprakriyā

Cleansing All States of Woe Tantra, Sarvadurgatiparisodhanatejorāja-nāma-mahākalparāja

Clusters of Quintessential Instructions, Śrīsaṃpuṭatantrarājaṭīkā āmnayamañjarī

Clusters Concerning Vajrayāna Downfalls, Vajrayānāpattimañjarī

Commentary on Difficult Points to Do with Root Downfalls, rTsa ltung bka' 'grel

Commentary on [Dīpaṃkarabhadra's] Guhyasamāja Maṇḍala Ritual in four hundred and fifty lines, *Śrīguhyasamājamaṇḍalavidhiṭīka*

Commentary on Great Vairocana's Enlightenment Discourse, Mahāvairocanābhisaṃbodhivikurvitādhiṣṭhānavaipulyasūtrendrarāja-nāma-dharma-paryāyabhāṣya

Commentary on the Black Yamāri Tantra, Kṛṣṇayamāritantrasya pañjikā ratvāvalī-nāma

Commentary on the Black Yamāri Tantra, Śrīyamāritantrapañjikāsahajālokanāma

Commentary on the Cleansing All States of Woe Tantra, Sarvadurgatipariśodhanatejorāja-nāma-mahākalparājasya ṭīkā

Commentary on the "Compendium of Principles," Ornament of Kosala, Kosalālaṃkāra-tattvasaṅgrahaṭīkā

Commentary on the "Compendium of Valid Cognitions," Pramāṇavārttikakārikā

Commentary on the Difficult Points of the Buddhakapāla Tantra Called Jñānavatī, Śrībuddhakapālatantrasya pañjikā jñānavatī nāma

Commentary on the Difficult Points of the Saṃvarodaya Tantra Pleasing to the Heroic Ones, Śrīcakrasaṃvarasya pañjikā śūramanojñā

Commentary on the Net of Illusion Tantra, Māyājālamahātantrarājaṭīkā

Commentary on the Root Downfalls, Vajrayānamūlāpattiṭīkā

Commentary on the Vajraḍāka Tantra, Śrīvajraḍāka-nāma-mahātantrarājasya ṭīkā

Compendium of All the Pledge Rituals, Dam tshig kun gyi cho ga kun las 'dus pa

Compendium of All the Pledges, Sarvasamayasaṅgraha

Continuation of the Explanation of the Saṃvara Tantra, Abhidhānottaratantra

Crown Jewel of the Guhyasamāja Tantra, 'Dus pa'i rin po che tog

Ḍākārṇava Yoginī Tantra, Śrīḍākārṇavamahāyoginītantrarāja-nāma

Engaging in the Bodhisattva Deeds, Bodhisattvacaryāvatāra

Exclusion of the Two Vajrayāna Extremes, Vajrayānakoṭidvayāpoha

Explanation of the Empowerment, Sekaprakriyā

Explanation of the Root and Branch Pledges [Sakya Pandita], Rdo rje theg pa'i rtsa ba dang yan lag gi dam tshig bshad pa

Exposition of "Reality Shining Like a Jewel," Tattvaratnālokavyākhyāna

Fearless Footsteps, Śrībuddhakapālamahātantrarājaṭīkā abhayapaddhatī

Fifty Stanzas on the Guru, Gurupañcāśatikā

Five Pledges, Samayapañca

Five Stages, Pañcakrama

Great Vairocana's Enlightenment Discourse, Mahāvairocanābhisaṃbodhi-vikurvitādhiṣṭhānavaipulyasūtrendrarāja-nāma-dharmaparyāya

Gross Downfalls, Sthūlāpatti

Guhyasamāja Panacea, gSang ba 'dus pa'i stong thun

Guhyasamāja Tantra, Sarvatathāgatakāyavākcittarahasyaguhyasamāja-nāma-mahākalparāja

Handful of Flowers Commentary, Kusumañjalīguhyasamājanibandhana

Hevajra Maṇḍala Ritual, Hevajramaṇḍalavidhi

Illuminating Lamp Commentary, Pradīpoddyotana-nāma-ṭīkā

Illumination of the "Compendium of Principles," Sarvatathāgatatattvasaṅgraha-mahāyānābhisamaya-nāmatantravyākhyā Tattvālokakarī

In Service to the Ultimate, Śrīparamārthasevā

Introduction to the Meaning of the Tantras, Tantrārthāvatāra

Jewel Lamp Commentary on the Black Yamāri Tantra, Śrīkṛṣṇayamārimahātantrarājapañjikāratnapradīpa-nāma

Kālacakra Tantra, Paramādibuddhoddhṛtaśrīkālacakra-nāma-tantrarāja

Lakṣmīṅkara's Root Downfalls Commentary, Vajrayānacaturdaśamūlāpattivṛtti

Lamp to View the Path, Kṛṣṇayamāritantrarājaprekṣaṇapathapradīpa-nāma-ṭīkā

Lamp Uniting One to the Practice, Caryāmelāpakapradīpa

Life of Tsongkhapa, Tsong kha pa chen po'i rnam thar

Light Garland of the Three Codes, Trisaṃvaraprabhāmālā

Light on the Tantric Way, Mantranayāloka

List of Texts Received, gSen yig

Little Saṃvara Tantra, Tantrarājaśrīlaghusaṃbhara-nāma

Long Śrīparamādya Commentary, Śrīparamādiṭīkā

Mahāmāyā Maṇḍala Ritual, Mahāmāyāmaṇḍalavidhi

Maṇḍala Ritual (Nāgabodhi), Śrīguhyasamāja-maṇḍalopāyikāviṃśatividhi-nāma

Maṇḍala Ritual of the Protectress with the White Parasol, Āryatathāgatoṣṇīṣa-sitātapatrāparājitā-nāma-maṇḍalavidhi

Mañjuśrī Root Tantra, Mañjuśrīmūlatantra

Ornament for the Essence, Śrīsarvaguhyavidhigarbhālaṃkāra

Ornament of the Guhyasamāja Tantra, Śrīguhyasamājālaṃkāra-nāma

Ornament for the Mahāyāna Sūtras, Mahāyānasūtrālaṃkārakārikā

Ornament of the Sage's Thought, Munimatālaṃkāra

Ornament of the Vajra Essence Tantra, Vajrahṛdayālāṃkāratantra

Ornamental Spot of Wisdom Tantra, Śrījñānatilakayoginītantrarāja-parama-mahābhūtam

Padminī Commentary on the Saṃvarodaya Tantra, Saṃvarodayamahā-tantrarājasya padminī-nāma-pañjikā

Pledges in Brief and at Length, Dam tshig mdo rgyas

Precious Garland of Advice for the King, Rājaparikathāratnāvalī

Ratnāvalī Commentary, [mDor byas pa'i] 'grel pa rin phreng

Reality Shining Like a Jewel, Tattvaratnāloka

Red Yamāri Maṇḍala Ritual, Śrīraktayamārimaṇḍalopāyikā

Red Yamāri Tantra, Śrīraktayamāritantrarāja-nāma

Ritual Evocation of the One Who Owns the Entire Doctrine, Śasanasarvasvaka-sādhana

Root Downfalls Commentary [Dragpa Gyeltsen], rTsa ba'i ltung ba bcu bzhi pa'i 'grel pa gsal byed 'khrul pa spong ba

Samāntabhadra Ritual Evocation, Samāntabhadra-nāma-sādhana

Saṃpuṭa Tantra, Saṃpuṭi-nāma-mahātantra

Saṃvara Maṇḍala Ritual, Śrīcakrasaṃvaramaṇḍalopāyikāratnapradīpodyota-nāma

Saṃvarodaya Tantra, Śrīmahāsaṃvarodayatantrarāja-nāma

Secret Ornamental Moon Spot Tantra, Śrīcandraguhyatilaka-nāma-mahātan-trarāja

Six Face Yamāri Tantra, Yamārikṛṣṇakarmasarvacakrasiddhakara-nāma-tantra-rāja

Skillful Means Sūtra, Upāyakauśalya-nāma-mahāyānasūtra

Śrīparamādya Tantra, Śrīparamādyamantrakalpakhaṇḍarāja

Stainless Light Commentary, Vimalaprabhā-nāma-mūlatantrānusāriṇī-dvadaśa-sāhasrikālaghukālacakratantrarājaṭīkā

Stream of Faith, Dad pa'i 'jug ngogs

Summary of Beginner's Pledges, Prathamakarmasamayasūtrasaṃgraha

Susiddhi Tantra, Susiddhikaramahātantrasādhanopāyikāpaṭala

Sūtra About What Is Important for Bhikṣus, Bhikṣuprarejusūtra-nāma

Three Heaps Sūtra, Āryatriskandha-nāma-mahāyānasūtra

Three Pledges Array Tantra, Trisamayavyūharāja-nāma-tantra

Trailokyavijaya Tantra Commentary, Āryatrailokyavijaya-nāma-vṛtti

Treasury of Knowledge, Abhidharmakośakārikā

Treasury of Secrets, Guhyakośa

Treatise on Pleasure, Kāmaśāstra

Vajra Tent Tantra, Āryaḍākinīvajrapañjara-nāma-mahātantrarājakalpa

Vajra Tip Tantra, Vajraśekharamahāguhyayogatantra

Vajra Verses Explaining the Kālacakra Consecration, Śrīkālacakratantrarājasya sekaprakriyāvṛttivajrapadodghaṭi

Vajrāvalī of Maṇḍala Rituals, Vajrāvalī-nāma-maṇḍalopāyikā

Vajraḍāka Tantra, Śrīvajraḍāka-nāma-mahātantrarāja

Vajraḍākinī Saṃvara Continuation Tantra, Śṛīsarvabuddhasamayogaḍākinī-jālasaṃbhara-nāmottaratantra

Vajradhātu Mahāmaṇḍala of the Compendium of Principles, Vajradhātu-mahā-maṇḍalopāyikāsarvavajrodaya-nāma-piṇḍārtha

Vajramālā, Śrīvajramālābhidhānamahāyogatantrasarvatantrahṛdayarahasya-vibhaṅga

Vajrayāna Gross Downfalls, Vajrayānasthūlāpatti

Vajrayāna Root Downfalls, Vajrayānamūlāpatti

Yoginī Tantra Called an Ornamental Spot of Mahāmudrā, Śrīmahāmudrā-tilakaṃ nāma yoginītantrarājādhipati

Index

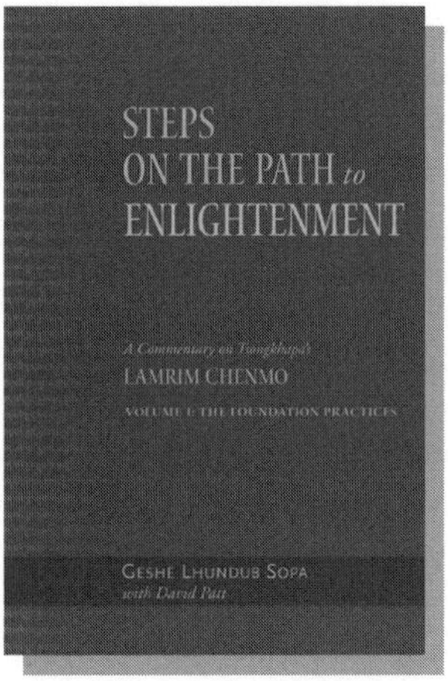

Steps on the Path to Enlightenment
A Commentary on the
Lamrim Chenmo, Volume 1
Geshe Lhundub Sopa
Foreword by His Holiness the Dalai Lama
608 pages, cloth ISBN 0-86171-346-X, $39.95

Volume I of an authoritative five-volume commentary on the *Lamrim Chenmo.* In the *Lamrim Chenmo,* Tsonghkapa explains the path in terms of the three levels of practitioners: those of small capacity who seek happiness in future lives, those of medium capacity who seek liberation from the cycle of suffering, and those of great capacity who seek full enlightenment in order to benefit al beings. This volume covers the topics common to the first level: Tsongkhapa's explanations of the role of the teacher, his exhortation to make the most of human existence, the contemplation of death and future lives, and going for the refuge.

Given his vast knowledge and his experience in both Tibetan and Western contexts, Geshe Sopa is the ideal commentator for this work for the modern student of Tibetan Buddhism.

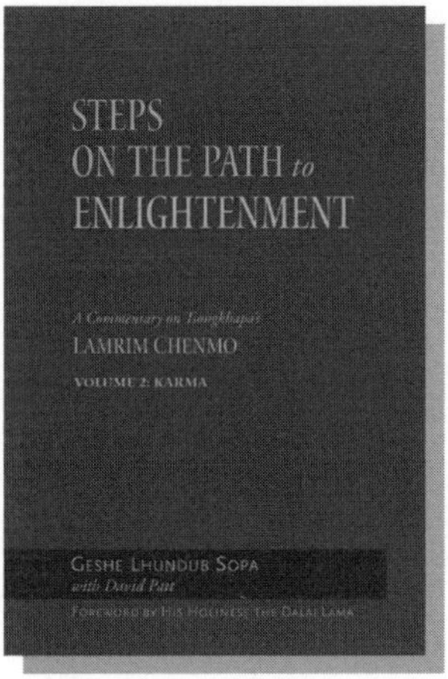

Steps on the Path to Enlightenment
A Commentary on the
Lamrim Chenmo, Volume 2: Karma
Geshe Lhundub Sopa with David Patt
512 pages, cloth, ISBN 0-86171-481-4, $29.95

The most comprehensive treatment of the key concept of karma yet published.

"Those fortunate to have studied directly with Geshe Sopa well know what an inexhaustible font of Buddhist learning and wisdom he is. With the publication of volume 2 of his comprehensive commentary on Tsongkhapa's classic *Lamrim Chemmo,* a much wider audience will further benefit from these unending riches. This text will appeal to practitioners and teachers alike for its crystal-clear presentation, in a direct and down-to-earth style, of one of the great encyclopedic texts of Tibetan Buddhism."—William S. Waldron, Associate Professor, Dept. of Religion, Middlebury College

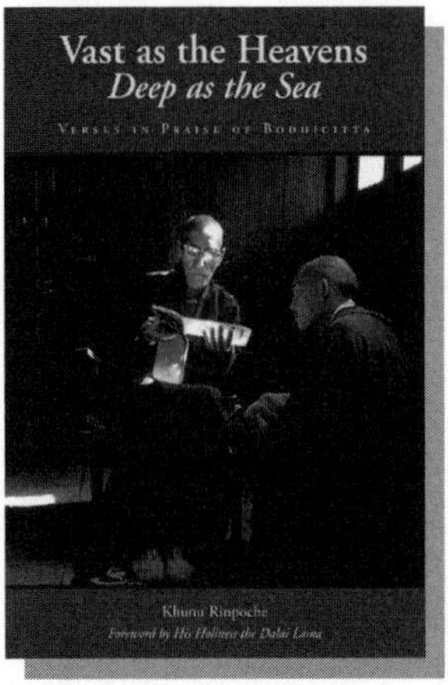

Vast as the Heavens, Deep as the Sea
Verses in Praise of Bodhicitta
Khunu Rinpoche
160 pages, ISBN 0-86171-146-7, $16.95

"Khunu Rinpoche was a bodhisattva and a saint. When I first heard of his *Praise of Bodhicitta,* I was filled with joy: what could be more precious than a teaching on bodhicitta by someone such as him? To hold in your hands Khunu Rinpoche's own words on bodhicitta is to be given a priceless opportunity—of touching the heart of a master who made it the guiding light of his entire life."—Sogyal Rinpoche, author of *The Tibetan Book of Living and Dying*

Practicing the Path
A Commentary on the Lamrim Chenmo
Yangsi Rinpoche
Foreword by Geshe Lhundub Sopa
576 pages, ISBN 0-86171-346-X, $24.95

A complete commentary on the *Lamrim Chenmo* in a single volume. Yangsi Rinpoche, a young tulku with the full training of a Tibetan scholar, here demonstrates his ability to teach directly to the Western mind. Beautifully edited and enjoyable to read, this is an excellent resource for those studying and meditating on the *lamrim,* the steps on the path to enlightenment.

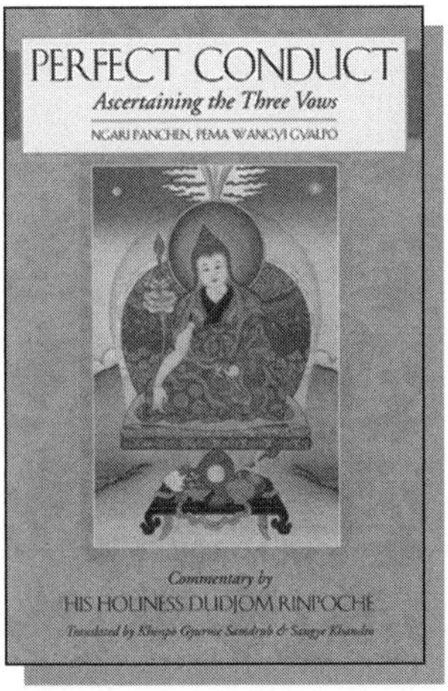

Perfect Conduct
Ascertaining the Three Vows
Commentary by His Holiness
Dudjom Rinpoche
192 pages, ISBN 0-86171-083-5, $18.00

"This book fulfills a crucial need for serious students of Buddhism. At last we have a handbook in English that explains the full code of discipline [pratimoksa, bodhisattva, and tantric vows]...along with an elucidation of...philosophical principles and the historical background."—from the preface by Tulku Thondup, author of *Hidden Teachings of Tibet*

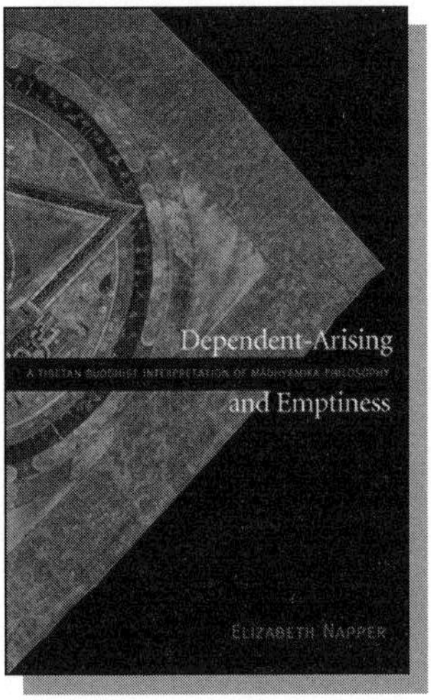

Dependent Arising and Emptiness
A Tibetan Buddhist Interpretation of Madhyamika Philosophy
Elizabeth Napper
868 pages, ISBN 0-86171-364-8, $29.95

"Through a detailed study of Tsongkhapa's understanding of emptiness and his critiques of rival interpretations, Elizabeth Napper examines the Tibetan interpretation of Nagarjuna's highly influential Middle Way philosophy. A must for anyone who is interested in Madhyamaka philosophy."—Thupten Jinpa, principal translator to H.H. the Dalai Lama and the author of *Self, Reality and Reason in Tibetan Philosophy: Tsongkhapa's Quest for the Middle Way*

The Fulfillment of All Hopes
Guru Devotion in Tibetan Buddhism
Tsongkhapa
Translated and introduced by Gareth Sparham
160 pages, ISBN 0-86171-153-X, $15.95

Devoting oneself to a spiritual teacher is a practice much misunderstood in the West, yet fundamental to the tantric Buddhism of Tibet. *The Fulfillment of All Hopes* is a complete translation of Lama Tsongkhapa's commentary on the well-known *Fifty Stanzas on the Guru,* accompanied by the original Tibetan text.

The Splendor of an Autumn Moon
The Devotional Verse of Tsongkhapa
Translated by Gavin Kilty
224 pages, ISBN 0-86171-192-0, $16.95

Here, presented in both the original Tibetan and in English translation, are twenty-one devotional poems by Tsongkhapa. Each verse—dedicated to the Buddha, bodhisattvas, and lamas—illuminates an aspect of the Buddhist path. Gavin Kilty's commentary places each prayer into context, and his careful, artful translations will appeal to anyone with a love of poetry.

About Wisdom

WISDOM PUBLICATIONS, a nonprofit publisher, is dedicated to making available authentic Buddhist works for the benefit of all. We publish translations of the sutras and tantras, commentaries and teachings of past and contemporary Buddhist masters, and original works by the world's leading Buddhist scholars. We publish our titles with the appreciation of Buddhism as a living philosophy and with the special commitment to preserve and transmit important works from all the major Buddhist traditions.

To learn more about Wisdom, or to browse books online, visit our website at wisdompubs.org. You may request a copy of our mail-order catalog online or by writing to this address:

Wisdom Publications
199 Elm Street
Somerville, Massachusetts 02144 USA
Telephone: (617) 776-7416
Fax: (617) 776-7841
Email: info@wisdompubs.org
www.wisdompubs.org

THE WISDOM TRUST

As a nonprofit publisher, Wisdom is dedicated to the publication of fine Dharma books for the benefit of all sentient beings and dependent upon the kindness and generosity of sponsors in order to do so. If you would like to make a donation to Wisdom, please do so through our Somerville office. If you would like to sponsor the publication of a book, please write or email us at the address above.

Thank you.

Wisdom is a nonprofit, charitable 501(c)(3) organization affiliated with the Foundation for the Preservation of the Mahayana Tradition (FPMT).